Janae

Thank you for coming over
and doing my hair. I haven't
driven a car in about 8 years,
haven't walked in years.
Thank you for your Kindness.
Blessings to you and I'm
Praying for you.

xxooo

Camille

UNPROTECTED

—— *Failures of General Motors and the UAW* ——

CAMILLE F. MCMILLAN

©Camille F. McMillan 2018

Print ISBN: 978-1-54394-515-7

eBook ISBN: 978-1-54394-516-4

All names in this book are Pseudonyms except the attorneys, judges and few agencies.

Dedicated to

Alyssa " Aliza Bracha " and George "Eliezer Gur"

and in memory of

Linda Gilbert, a Chrysler Millwright, who was brutally harassed at Chrysler Motor Company and whom the company, the UAW, and the courts and also failed.

ACKNOWLEDGEMENTS

The Canadians

Sandy Feldheim who began the editing. I met her and she volunteered her services to help shape my book. She also introduced me to my editor Feral Sage. Thank you Sandy.

Feral Sage was my editor. We spent many hours on Skype together. She really shaped my book for me.

Steve Izma who is a Canadian publisher. He took the time out of his busy day to read my book and offer his opinion.

The Americans

Micki Grossman who is a personal family friend who read my book. She is a highly intelligent woman and I value her opinions.

David Schied who was also a reader. He produced a series on me called "Power Corrupts Again."

Muriel Broomfield who is my very intelligent sister. She read for me twice.

Temple Israel is my place of worship. I have never felt my skin color there. Temple Israel Sisterhood has helped me to renew my faith in humanity. They are the finest women that I have ever met.

CHAPTER 1

I was the youngest child of five, born in 1956. I have two brothers and two sisters. Times were hard then for Black America. The Civil Rights movement was just beginning. My father left the family when I was about three, and my mother had to raise five children with minimal support. It was a different era and a woman with children could do virtually nothing without a husband. We were poor, as were most of our neighbors.

I was not aware of our poverty because we had the richness of family. We would take long walks through the neighborhoods together. To us kids, it was an adventure, but I now think it was my mom's way to tire us out so she could get some much-needed rest. Mom kept an immaculate house, even with five children to tend. She was also a great cook and had the gift of being able to turn shoe leather into something tender and pleasing to the palate.

Because my mother received minimal support from my father, we had to rely on Aid to Dependent Children. It almost killed the proud woman she was. My mother had been a hard working woman even before she was married and had children. She had depended on my father to support the family and hadn't been used to relying on others. When he left us without support, she had to accept help from the state. This was totally embarrassing to her, but she had children to feed.

When a social worker told her she would have to move us to the projects in downtown Detroit, she resisted. In these housing projects, females were more vulnerable to assault, and she had three daughters. Our landlord was a nice Jewish man from Germany, and he came to her rescue. He liked the way she tended his property and kept it clean and neat. The grass was always cut and the trash picked up. Our landlord asked her to stay and told her he would work with her on the rent. My mother never forgot his kindness.

Ours was a family-friendly neighborhood. Everyone looked out for everyone else. Kids were respectful of adults and feared their parents' wrath. Strict discipline was necessary to ensure that children obeyed the law in order to keep them alive. Raising Black males during that era was especially difficult. My mother had two Black sons to nurture to adulthood. In 1967, following widespread rioting, Detroit police had created a task force called STRESS, which was an acronym for "Stop the Robberies, Enjoy Safe Streets." It was a controversial unit, and many Black males did not fare well under it. In four years 17 civilians had been killed by STRESS. One officer killed three people in six years and injured nine others. The STRESS unit was finally disbanded in 1974. Without the support of a male role model, my mother had to teach my brothers responsibility from an early age.

We were living in the heart of the city when the 1967 riots broke out. On July 23, 1967, the Detroit police raided a "blind pig," which is an illegal drinking establishment. The patrons had been celebrating the return of two Vietnam veterans. Everyone was arrested. This set off a riot. Somehow, Jews were blamed for the unrest, and Jewish-owned businesses were looted and burned. Mom couldn't understand the hate directed at the Jews; her landlord had been so kind.

I remember when Mom heard a noise in the middle of the night and fearfully peered out the front window. A spotlight hit her in the face. The National Guard was driving down our street in tanks. Thankfully, she was not mistaken for a sniper and shot. It was a frightening time for all of us. We kids were restricted to the front porch.

We moved to a new, predominantly White area after the riots, and my mother remarried. Papa, as I call him, was a wonderful man. He treated my Mom well and looked out for us kids. We felt safe and secure with him around. We were one of few Black families in the area. Our neighbors were nice, although they did have a "Little Black Sambo" mascot designed as a lawn watering device. "Sambo" held the hose as it slowly jerked back and forth. Even so, I grew to love that family. The mother taught me how to knit. Over time, the neighborhood changed into a Black neighborhood, and "Little Black Sambo" was painted white.

Considering that this was the late sixties, I was fortunate not to experience too many racial incidents. The Jewish kids in my neighborhood had it just as bad as the Black kids. I remember walking home from school and seeing a crowd of kids ahead of me. And then I witnessed a deplorable act. A Jewish girl, a little older than I, was being tortured by the kids because of her stereotypical Jewish features and because she was brainy. They mocked her mercilessly. I'll always remember the tears streaming down her face as she tried to escape. I ran away before they could turn on me. Her family moved shortly after that incident.

In school I pursued college prep courses, intending to become a Certified Public Accountant. I was shy and tried to overcome this by playing tennis and basketball as extra-curricular activities. Basketball was harder for me, but I excelled at tennis and was All-City in 1974. I experienced my first major illness in September of that year, with a bout of mononucleosis causing me to miss the first two weeks of school. I was devastated. I lived for school. When I recovered, I tried to play basketball again, despite my doctor's warning that my enlarged spleen, a result of the illness, could rupture. I was determined not to quit. Although my coach was aware of the risk, she kept me on the team and even allowed me a little playing time towards the end of the season.

While I was in high school, my mother attended night college. I went to her classes with her and did my homework there. Her math professors loved me. They would administer their tests to the class and to me. I always aced the tests; my brain is wired for math. My mother later graduated from the University of Alabama with a teaching degree.

I graduated from high school in January, 1975, at the top of my class. I was class president and valedictorian. I planned to attend college, but I desperately needed a job. Although I had won a four year scholarship to a major university, it did not include room and board. My parents moved south two weeks after my graduation. I was now an adult and needed a means of supporting myself. I began school and, since I had four years of sewing experience in high school, applied at General Motors to work as a Sewer, sewing the seat cushions and other things in the interior of the car.

I entered the plant in April of 1976. There were about thirteen of us in my group. We were led to our work areas by a general foreman, who instructed me to stand off to the side while other supervisors (also known as foremen) chose the workers they wanted to work for them. In the plant, the supervisor, or foreman, is the lowest level of management. Above the supervisor (foreman) are the general foreman, the superintendent, and the area manager. Each position controls the one below in rank.

The general foreman escorted me to an area commonly known as "behind the wall," where I met my supervisor, Mr. Littleton*. I was the only

Black person in this group of new hires, and he was not pleased that I had been hired for this job. He placed me on a job called "tack-down." It was simple enough. You marry the material to the foam and sew around the edges to hold it in place.

The rule of thumb was that you had to make 80% of production within three days to keep your job. I was already at 80% within the first half of the day when the supervisor placed me on a job called "one needle design sew." I worked this job, and once again I was making 80%. On Thursday, when I reported to work, he moved me again. This time he placed me on a job called "pay-point." In this operation, the seat cushions are sewn with extra precise details added to them. There may be several layers of material added. Pay-point was the hardest job in the department, and even the most experienced operators had difficulty with it. I saw regular operators with years of experience looking at each other, perplexed. They were horrified for me.

The day after I was hired, a pretty, White woman around my age also joined the department. She took long breaks and long lunches, and did virtually no work. My supervisor smiled and laughed with her although she was not making anywhere near production. That Friday was Good Friday, and we were off for the holiday. When I returned to work on Monday, I was once again placed on the pay-point job. A little later, my supervisor told me to accompany him. He said something to the newly hired checker (an employee who delivers the work to the operators). The checker looked panicked while Mr. Littleton was speaking with him. Then I saw him pick up the yellow "production standard" cards, write something on them, and hand them to Mr. Littleton.

Mr. Littleton then presented me to Labor Relations with these cards. He wanted to lay me off on the grounds that I was "unable to perform job available." He and Labor Relations had an argument, and I heard the labor rep say, "I'm getting tired of this." Of course, I had no idea what he meant, but I was soon to find out. Apparently, the checker had written up production cards on me that did not give an accurate accounting of my week's work. My work pieces were being used to fatten up the other girl's count. As for the pieces I had done on pay-point, the checker had not even been near me in hours, although he produced a card stating that I had only sewn seven pieces per hour. It was a total fabrication.

If a supervisor insists on a discipline, Labor Relations has to issue it. In the end, Labor Relations had to yield to the supervisor, and I lost my job. It was the beginning of a long education with General Motors. They had the audacity to ask me to sign a paper stating, "I agree this is the reason for this separation." Of course, I did not sign the statement. I've been cautious about what I sign ever since. I went home that day and cried myself to sleep. The next morning I woke up and darted off to college, still very upset. I made up my mind, in school, that I was not going to just sit back and accept this type of injustice. After school, I rode three buses to the Michigan Department of Civil Rights and filed a complaint. They began an investigation into the matter.

Since I had only worked approximately one week, I was not entitled to union representation. Unbeknownst to me, the women in my department, Black and White, had summoned their union rep. These wonderful women were appalled that the company continued to tolerate this situation, and agreed to testify for me. As it turned out, I was the fourth Black person in four weeks that Mr. Littleton had fired. After I filed my complaint, Mr. Littleton took a medical leave. Upon his return, a Civil Rights investigator from the Michigan Department of Civil Rights visited him. The investigator, a Black man, told me that while speaking with him, Mr. Littleton had said inappropriate and disrespectful things. (He reported what was said to the Michigan Department of Civil Rights, but not to me.) This supervisor did not have the mindset to hide his hatred of minorities even when speaking with a Civil Rights advocate. He saw skin color only.

GM reinstated me, but without back pay for lost time. I also lost six months seniority. In the land of the factory, seniority means everything. Lay-offs, even for extremely long periods, are your burden to bear, and are sometimes determined just by the first letter of your last name. Even if you were hired on the same date as another employee, your seniority was determined by your last name. A-Z was high seniority in the even years, and Z-A in odd number years.

The hourly personnel director, Mr. Springfield, asked me upon my return, "You're the one who was discriminated against?"

I replied, "Yes."

"Well, we don't want that now, do we?" I spent the next thirteen years at the Fisher Body plant without too many incidents, considering the era. There are always going to be some people who look for a reason to hate and blame others for their problems. This usually stems, in my opinion, from low self-worth, fear, and ignorance.

My next significant altercation with management came about because of a Black woman. I was working one day while two important members of our bargaining committee were on the floor. They were looking for someone to represent the employees for the day. The regular union steward was in meetings, and they had to have someone on the floor. They spotted me and thought that I might be strong enough to attempt to do the job. I concurred. This became my introduction to the workings of the union and the prelude to my first "write-up."

A write-up is a written discipline issued by your supervisor. The first discipline is verbal, the second is written, and the third results in suspension without pay. For serious infractions of the rules, suspension without pay is immediate. Labor Relations almost always did what the supervisor wanted. My supervisor was a tall, powerfully-built, religious, Black woman. She towered over all the women in the department. Her very size was frightening. I was young and naive, and she had daughters my age. She wanted to advance in the company, and decided that the way to do it would be to go after the Black union rep. As everyone knows, in a fight, if you take out the presumed leader first the rest of the pack will probably take flight. Life in the plant is tough, and only the strong survive. I wanted to survive, so I had to become strong. I wasn't a leader; I was just standing up for myself.

The regular committee person, also known as a union rep, was off for the day. As her alternate, I was scheduled to work the floor in her absence and answer committee calls. Union reps are the people from the union who represent employees in front of management. The supervisor had 24 hours advance notice that I was to work the floor, and knew that she had to relieve me of my duties after two hours.

When the time came for me to return to the floor, I asked her for my replacement. She became angry and turned the line off to curse me out. She had an audience for her performance. If you work in a factory, you know that the assembly line is *never* turned off unless there is an emergency. She expected me to back down, but I stood up to her, which surprised her. The rest of the employees were watching in astonishment. She was so angry, she was clenching her fist. It seemed as if she wanted to hit me; but I had the drill motor I was working with in my hand. Had she attacked me, I'd have been forced to use it. She turned the line back on and sent my relief person over, but she made me her pet project after that.

Every day I worked, she watched me like a hawk. She tried to find errors in any job I was doing. I was a relief person, which meant I had to be able to handle all the jobs. She would assign me to different jobs and constantly check my work. It took her about a month, but she was finally able to frame me for "Careless Workmanship." Doors were going through the system with no glue on the top edge and the other workers couldn't do their job. It was a mechanical fault, but she blamed me; and that's all she needed to do when she presented me to Labor Relations. Labor Relations left my case pending for one day because they didn't believe her. Again, the supervisor insisted upon disciplinary action and Labor Relations had to abide by her wishes. After I received the write-up, I passed it around the line for all the girls to see. This "good Christian" supervisor, as she referred to herself, could not believe I was letting the other workers see it. They knew it was a complete fabrication and that I had nothing to hide.

I wrote grievances against this supervisor, and when the time came to settle them, I was able to attend the meeting with my "zone man." (The zone man oversees the committee person.) At first, the superintendent, Jason Eastman, berated me. Then he told me that, although I could not discipline GM managers, they could discipline me. But Jason was fair in his dealings with me.

I asked him, "You know Christine Liley don't you?" Christine was a coworker and alternate committee person.

He nodded, "Yes."

"You know she won't lie for either one of us then."

He knew this to be true, and said he would send for her. At this point, the supervisor started stammering, asking him to send for someone else who was a friend of hers. He knew then she was lying. He told her that she was the one playing games, not me.

He said to me, "Let me get this garbage off your record right now. I knew something was wrong when I saw 'Careless Workmanship.' I laughed when I saw the write-up." He removed the write-up from my record. I didn't receive another discipline for 16 years, until I arrived at the Pontiac Assembly Center

CHAPTER 2

As I look back, I can see that the signs of Multiple Sclerosis were becoming apparent as early as 1978 and 1979. I experienced periods where my right thigh would burn for no apparent reason. Packing it in ice did not help. The fire was within. After a few days, it would subside. These incidents would occur at different intervals over the years. I also had bouts of weakness and fatigue, but I was young and refused to dwell on it.

My husband and I met during Christmas of 1977. He was in his last semester of college and had played college football. He was educated, respectful of women, and not biased against any group of people. He also had the most beautiful set of white teeth. I was attracted.

We married in September, 1982. Both of us had moved in diverse social circles, and this was reflected in our wedding. Our guests were from varied backgrounds, races, and religions. One friend told me she was not coming to the wedding because White people would be there. I told her I would miss her because we would not tolerate other people's race issues at our wedding. Our White friends were not going to be uninvited because a Black friend didn't like White people.

My husband and I decided to start a family two years later, and in 1985 I had a beautiful daughter, born 10 weeks premature. After we brought her home, I began experiencing strange physical symptoms. Sometimes when

I would stand, my legs would buckle beneath me. One morning when I got out of bed, my legs failed me completely and I collapsed on the floor. I crawled back into bed and waited another ten minutes before attempting to get up again; but the same thing happened. When I was finally able to stand, I proceeded to take my shower, and told my husband I was going to the hospital. He wanted to accompany me, but it was cold outside and I didn't want to take the baby out. I made it to the hospital and parked in the emergency lot, but when I exited my vehicle, I fell to the cold ground. Scared and frustrated, I crawled back into the car. I attempted a second time and the same thing happened. Eventually, I made it inside the hospital. The emergency doctor could only diagnose a bladder infection. He prescribed antibiotics.

In January 1986, I returned to work after an eight-month layoff, reporting to an area known as J-Doors. (The auto factories commonly name work areas using the alphabet.) J-Doors assembled the interior of the car doors. The supervisor was a man named Fred, and he was quite a nasty character. He seemed to be insecure about his height because he would say things to us like, "Shit runs downhill, and it's going to run all over you." His other favorite expression was, "When I get through standing on your shoulders, you're going to think I'm ten feet tall."

Fred treated all the Black employees poorly and addressed us as "Hey, you." He catered to two White women in my department, while he treated my Black partner and me like garbage. I worked on one side of the door and she worked on the other. In every work area there was a designated place to smoke. Three people were allowed to use the smoke bench at one time, and for no more than 10 minutes. Fred allowed the White women to sit at the smoke bench for long periods. He would laugh with them, smirking at my partner and me because we were loaded with work. He should have distributed some work to them to meet production standards. In reality, he was not hurting anyone but the company. Fortunately, our local union was strong and tried to get justice for everyone regardless of color. The union leadership did not seem to have deeply ingrained racial, religious or gender-based biases. After the union presented a letter that I wrote to the area superintendent addressing Fred's abusive behavior, Fred toned down his attitude.

One day I was happily working when I remembered that I needed to speak to a union rep who was working in an office above me about an upcoming union bowling event. After visiting Keith, I descended the stairs. Halfway down, my legs cramped and locked up on me. I continued down the steps on willpower and fear. I have no idea how I made it to my work-station, but when I returned there my body felt as though it wanted to retreat to a fetal position. My left arm folded over like a lobster claw. Over my protests, my partner started yelling for someone from the plant medical department to call the ambulance. I visited the plant medical department and obtained a pass to visit my own doctor. My doctor thought I had low potassium, and prescribed medication. The episodes faded. I was later laid off from October, 1989 until March, 1993 because of a downturn in vehicles being ordered.

On March 15, 1993, General Motors recalled me to work after an almost four year layoff. I reported to the Saginaw Gear and Axle Detroit plant. My first supervisor was a formidable-looking man. Although initially he frightened me, I soon came to have nothing but respect for him. He treated me well, and I tried to work hard for him. My job was difficult and hard on my body, but I loved it. I started construction of the axles by placing parts on the axle shafts before a machine placed sealant on the axle and pressed the parts together. This made the axles heavy. I lost 30 lbs in nine months without even trying because the job was so fast paced. This was a good weight loss.

When I first arrived at the GM Gear and Axle plant the guys were all over me. Plants are known to be meat markets and I was the fresh supply. I had my own disgusting fan club. When GM sold the plant to American Axle in 1994, the word went around that a woman with green eyes was working in the plant. Only 2% of the world's population has green eyes. The guys came out like roaches at night. They would gather behind me and take bets on which man would have me first. They wouldn't mind passing me around. I know that they were taking bets because the guy who worked beside told me so. He, too, was trying to sleep with me and figured that he would eliminate the competition. I finally screamed at all of them to leave me alone and told them none of their ignorant behinds had a chance because I had a husband. They walked away mumbling that I was crazy, but they gawked at me from a distance.

One humid, late summer day, I felt an unsettling sensation while I was working. It was nothing I could explain, but I instinctively knew I needed time off. I had vacation days available, and my supervisor allowed me to take them. I lay in my bed for three days without any energy. The fourth day I woke up ready and able to return to work.

In July, applications for Skilled Trades positions were being accepted by management. Skilled trades maintain all the equipment and the buildings. One of the forklift drivers convinced me to submit an application. My friend of over 25 years, Milton, was submitting one. I figured I would know at least one man in the trades. When we filled out our applications, we were told by the Apprentice Coordinator not to take the test if we didn't feel comfortable taking it at that time. There was a brush-up course being offered at the local community college. It had been years since I'd been in school, but I didn't believe I'd have a problem.

After the test, I heard people all around me saying how well they had done, and that the test had been easy. I wondered if they had just taken the same test I had. The test was not easy. I felt I had passed, but didn't know where I stood. The apprentice coordinator later told me that the test was purposely hard. Previous applicants had passed the tests, but were not able to handle the schoolwork associated with the apprenticeship. Apprentices had to attend community college.

I normally worked 11 hours per night and did not arrive home until around 4:00 a.m. I would sleep a few hours, wake up, and get my daughter to school. When I returned home, I would go back to sleep. I was dead asleep when the phone rang. It was Linda from Labor Relations. My first thought was, What did I do to get fired? Labor Relations had never called me at home. Linda told me that we had a situation to discuss. My heart raced. I squeaked out, "What situation?" She informed me that, because of my high test score, other than the pipefitting position, I would be able to choose my trade. I had received the highest score out of 900 applicants. She told me to make sure I contacted her as soon as I arrived at work, as the other positions needed to be filled properly by the test scores.

I fell back on the bed and closed my eyes. It took about five minutes for the full impact of what she had said to hit me. I sat straight up, not believing what I had just heard, and called her back immediately. I told her I wanted the Electrical position, and she affirmed that it was mine. When I arrived on the job, I ran into the Apprentice Coordinator. He was not happy I had taken the electrical job. I later learned he had promised it to a White male if he could get me to accept a Sheet Metal apprenticeship position.

On December 13, 1993, I began my career as a skilled tradesman. Along with five other apprentices, I reported to work as an apprentice electrician. The first week on the job was devoted to safety training. We covered lock-out, manlifts, fall safety, confined spaces, fire safety, and more. The first safety lesson was: "YOUR SAFETY IS YOUR RESPONSIBILITY. LOCK-OUT IS UP TO YOU." Lock-out is the process of bringing the equipment to zero energy so that nothing is able to move or electrocute any trades person or prevent unexpected machine movement.

After the week of safety training, the six apprentices reported to our respective areas. I will never forget the terror I felt as I entered into the electrical crib filled with men to begin my new life. I was standing there petrified, and no one said a word to me. They just stared at me. I wondered what I had gotten myself into. One man in particular was staring at me and smiling as if to say, *We've got you now*. A few minutes passed. An apprentice approached me and escorted me to an area where the other apprentices were standing. I was grateful for the rescue.

I was assigned to work with a journeyman by the name of Jacob. Apprentices are required to complete 7,328 hours on the job and 576 hours of school. Employees-in-training are required to spend more time on the job and less time in school. A journeyman, a fully qualified person, has completed 4-8 years of school and on the job training. Jacob was highly intelligent and a pleasure to work with. On the outside, he seemed gruff, but I adored him. He was more than willing to teach me everything he could.

After Jacob, I worked with Mac, also a wonderful man. We discussed how green I was. I lacked exposure to tools, fittings, and terminology; but Mac had a lot of patience and knowledge, and he did everything he could to train me to become an asset to the company. I found that if the men had knowledge to share and knew their trade well, they were willing to share what they knew and did not feel threatened by me. I asked that they treat me like one of the guys, but without the cursing, and got what I asked.

I knew it was easier for people to assume I had made it through because I was a Black female. That thought probably comforted individuals who had low self-esteem. Although I didn't get my job through Affirmative Action, I understand why Affirmative Action is needed. The playing field isn't level. My experience at Pontiac Truck Plant would soon prove that. I found the atmosphere to be both sexist and racist. I was called derogatory names and harassed for sex. The managers placed barriers in my way when I tried to go back to school to become an electrical engineer.

The men at the American Axle plant in Detroit were tough, but fair. Sometimes they would play jokes on me to test my inner strength. The journeymen would send me up for the elevator, then cut the power and trap me between the floors. It was a very old elevator. I had to walk to the floor where it had last stopped and get on to make it move again. If I walked past a manlift, they would make it backfire. They only wanted to make sure I didn't panic easily considering the work we were doing. Once, they took me up high in the building steel and left me in a nasty conveyor. The area was filthy, and the grime went through my heavy coveralls. Every inch of me was covered in black, gritty grease. My face looked like a coal miner's. I was elevated so high, everyone below looked like ants to me. When they got tired of me not working and not crying, they came back for me. Everyone laughed at my appearance. I was so filthy, one journeyman felt sorry for me.

"Camille, do you have more clean coveralls at Central?" he asked, as his eyes tried not to laugh at my grimy appearance.

"Yes, I have a couple of clean pairs."

"Do you want to go to back to Central and change into a clean pair?"

"Why? So you guys can take me back up there, get me filthy again, and laugh at me some more. No, thank you. I'm already dirty, so I'll wait until the shift is over." I earned much respect for not being afraid of the dirt or too concerned about my appearance.

My next assignment was to the construction gang. The construction crew built new devices in the plant. We ran wire and pipes for everything electrical, and also installed new machines. I had expected some resistance to my presence, but they included me. Two White male pipefitters gave me some of the best advice around. One guy told me, "Camille, always remember you can do this because it's made by man." The other was an older man who was soon to retire. He told me, "Hon, if the guys give you a hard time about taking a man's job, tell them you don't get a break on your bills because you're a woman."

One day as I was climbing down a ladder, when I got to the bottom a guy grabbed me by the hand and started brushing off the dirt from my thighs, saying that he hated seeing beautiful women dirty. I pushed him away from me and told him never to touch me again. He was the plant womanizer. Another man approached me while I was working. He was showing me all 32 teeth and trying to sweet talk me. I looked at him like he was crazy and told him that I was trying to learn something, that I was married, and to please not approach me again. I wasn't irresistible; I just had the right anatomy,

The only real trouble I recall when I was working with the men came at the hands of a newly-hired journeyman. GM had sold the Gear and Axle plant to a new group called American Axle in 1994. American Axle was hiring new employees. It was early in the morning and the sun was beginning to rise. Mac and I were traveling to a job in our plant vehicle, and stopped for a crossing train. There was a man on the sidewalk beside us. He said hello, focused in on me, and tried to flirt with me. I wasn't interested in talking. I don't make it a practice to hold conversations with strange men in the streets. We were in the heart of the city, and he could be anyone. A few weeks later, the man hired into the plant.

His name was Sam, and he let me know he had been the one talking to me at the railroad tracks. He thought I had snubbed him, and it was obvious he didn't understand why. I eventually found out that he was not used to women ignoring him. When they did, he gave them a hard time. After he was hired in as a journeyman he began to pursue me. Since I was an apprentice he had power over me and he stepped up his pursuit and his abuse. The sexual harassment from this man had an early beginning.

I occasionally had to work with Sam. He constantly tried to get my attention. My friend, Roy, told him to leave me alone because I was married and not interested. This meant absolutely nothing to Sam. A few weeks passed before I had to work with him again. He decided he would use this time to make me pay for my lack of interest in him. We climbed into the manlift. I was driving and working the controls. When we were high up in the building steel, an area above the equipment and accessible only by ladder or a manlift, he started to tell me what he had done with a woman the night before. I told him I didn't care to hear it.

He continued, "I can get any woman I want on the plant floor."

I said, "Knock yourself out."

He became angry and started making degrading statements about women to me. All during this time I smelled heavy alcohol on his breath and saw that his eyes were bloodshot. He told me he had arrived home at two in the morning from partying and drinking. I surmised that the alcohol was just starting to take effect since we started work at 6 a.m. and he was still reeking of it. Sam decided that, since I was captive in the manlift with him, he could describe his sex acts. I was flabbergasted. He had no respect for women. We were up in tight building steel, and he decided to critique my every move. I was moving the controls, and so was he. For safety reasons, only one person can drive a manlift at a time; so I sat down and let him take the controls. After a few minutes passed, he ordered me to drive again. When I got control of the lift, I began descending to safety.

He shouted, "Where are you going?"

I remained silent as I continued to descend. Sam snatched at the controls, but because of his inebriated state, he lost his balance. I hurriedly finished my descent and exited the lift. I told the other journeyman what had transpired, and refused to work with a drunk for the rest of the shift. I had the right to refuse to work with any employee in an unsafe condition. After our break, he said, "Are you scared to go up?"

"No."

He snarled, "Let's go."

"You are intoxicated and I refuse to subject myself to working with an employee in an unsafe condition."

That did not endear me to him. Apprentices usually do as they are told, but they do not have to subject themselves to unsafe working conditions. He became angrier. The other journeyman I was assigned to work with had witnessed this exchange and dispatched me to chase parts. He wanted to remove me totally from this man's presence.

Just after lunch, Sam demanded to talk to me. "You must trust me not to operate the equipment in an unsafe condition."

"I wouldn't trust my own husband if he were in an unsafe condition like you."

"I apologize for some of the things I said about women, but as far as my nasty attitude is concerned, you'll just have to eat my shit."

Shocked, I replied, "I don't know what type of women you normally deal with, but I'm not one of them."

I backed up and ran to stay beside the other journeyman. Being the only female working with men, you didn't want them to be afraid of working with you as you might file sexual harassment charges against them. Sometimes you may bump into each other in the wrong way. Sometimes guys had touched my breast accidentally, meaning no sexual disrespect. Women tradesmen try to keep the words "sexual harassment" from escaping their lips; but sexual harassment is what I was experiencing.

The following week, management transferred Sam to a different work area. I was thrilled to be rid of him, but my joy was short-lived. The next weekend I almost ended up working with him again and I saw him licking his chops as he glared at me. I think my leader, Jake, also saw this. He sent me to work with another seasoned journeyman. You could see a look of disappointment on Sam's face, and the relief on mine. A few weeks passed, and Sam was terminated for being intoxicated on the job. He had brought the termination upon himself, but I was relieved to be free of him. He came back a few weeks later working for a contractor. Some of the guys who saw him told me he was asking about me.

In those days, I would often travel with the apprenticeship committee to the inner city schools to speak about Skilled Trades. One of the things we cautioned the kids about was getting high. I always stressed to the students that if they drank or used drugs, I would not work with them. I would not jeopardize my safety.

CHAPTER 3

Things were going pretty well until June of 1994, when there was a fatality at the plant. It was near the end of the shift and, with just one quick repair to make to complete his job, a machine repairman had removed his safety lock from the equipment and entered the machine. The safety lock prevents the machine from being turned on. Seeing no lock, another employee energized the machine. The machine rotated and crushed the repairman's head.

Tradesmen bond like police officers and firefighters. Because of the hazardous conditions we face on our jobs, we try to look out for each other. The employee who lost his life was well-liked, and we felt terrible for his family. It was a reminder to me of the risks of the job, and how important it is to always apply proper lockout, no matter how quick the job may be.

On January 6, 1995, tragedy struck again. This time it was Regina, a female millwright, employee-in-training. Millwrights handle the moving of heavy equipment and the maintenance of the building. It was an extremely cold day, and Regina was dispatched to the roof of Plant 1 to close windows that had been left open by some employees who had been smoking weed. She fell through the window to the plant floor, striking her head on structural beams, and died. We were like family at "the Gear," so we were all devastated. Scheduled to work nine hours, I learned of Regina's death in the eighth. She and I shared a small locker room, and I sometimes tutored her in math. We went to Bible classes together on our lunch hour.

Electricians work with extremely dangerous equipment. For example, we had a high frequency induction heating machine that heated steel shafts up to such a high temperature they glowed cherry red. It had a huge capacitor. Capacitors store electrical energy, and some can be deadly. A journeyman by the name of Tom escorted me to the entrance panel of the machine and said, "Never open these doors while the machine is running. If you do, you're dead." The charge in the capacitors would leap out and kill me. For safety, it was necessary to use a ground stick, which discharges the excess energy while protecting the worker from a potentially lethal shock.

The morning after Regina's death, my supervisor, Nick Skrien, decided to conduct my performance appraisal. We sat in his office as he gave me his version of my training progress. This meeting was merely a formality because the supervisors do not work with you; your assigned journeyman does. The journeyman also fills out an evaluation. I was astonished when Nick said, "We want you to work by yourself."

Regina had lost her life less than 24 hours before, and now I was being ordered to work by myself. I was an apprentice with approximately 2,600 hours of working experience. Apprentices were required to complete 4,000 hours of training before they could work unsupervised, and new apprentices always had to work with a journeyman. To become a journeyman, an apprentice had to complete 7,328 hours of on-the-job training and 576 hours of school. I knew I was not ready to fly solo.

When I first entered the trades, Nick was an electrical leader and a former UAW official. Shortly after my arrival, he went into management. Electrical leaders oversee the electricians. They also plan and order all the supplies for the jobs. Nick had been President of our UAW local and knew all the hazards of the job. Having served in both management and union positions, he was aware of all the safeguards that apply to apprentices. He knew I should not work alone.

In our meeting I said, "Nick, I don't know what I am doing yet. I haven't had enough experience. Your three new journeymen, two White males and one White female, work together every day and they have over 30 years of combined experience." I wanted Nick to see that I saw the injustice of what he was doing. I knew he was trying to get me to quit. He replied, "I know, but we don't want you to be like them." Nick knew they were unqualified electricians. The female electrician had only wired panel boxes for a panel wiring company. She had never worked with live electricity, yet she had been given a journeyman's card. She came in as a journeyman and was supposed to have some knowledge of what she was doing; but my journeyman was training her at the same time as he was training me. She made it obvious that she resented my presence by casting nasty looks in my direction while I was being instructed.

The journeyman who was training me, along with the other apprentices and the new hires, was a Black man. Nick didn't care for him, even though he was the best electrician in Plant 3. I asked Nick what my journeyman felt about me working alone. He would only say, "Judging by what your journeyman says, you need to work alone." I asked him if my journeyman had told him that he didn't want to train me. He refused to answer that question. He only said, "I don't want you to go anywhere near a journeyman."

I called my Apprentice Coordinator. The coordinator came, and that's when I learned who was coaching Nick. It was Nick's supervisor, Reggie Bloom. My coordinator spoke with my journeyman, who insisted that I work with him. The two supervisors, the apprentice coordinator, and I had a meeting. Reggie finally said to me, "If you think you need a journeyman, you can have one and we won't think any less of you." I let him know I was aware that if anyone working in that plant should have a trainer, it should be me, the least experienced electrical apprentice. I really didn't care what they thought of me. This was a matter of my safety.

I believe that, knowing I was upset about Regina's death, they were trying to instill fear in me to force me out of the trades. I wrote up the incident because I knew they would make life difficult for me. Labor Relations stepped in, took control of the situation, and called supervisors Nick and Reggie Bloom on the carpet. They knew better, and their supervisor apologized to me. Labor Relations admonished the supervisor for ignoring plant policy and procedures, especially concerning safety. The situation was put to rest. I ended up cleaning out Regina's locker and returning her belongings to her brother, who also worked at the plant. It was an emotionally devastating experience.

I also began to experience more health problems in 1995. An OB/GYN informed me that I had fibroid tumors and would require a total hysterectomy. My time was too valuable to waste dwelling on it at that moment, so I chose to put off the surgery. I also needed to find a new doctor. My original doctor had moved and left her patients in another doctor's care. I wanted a doctor of my choosing.

In July, 1995, a journeyman sent me back to Central, the electrical crib housing all electrical parts, to bring some electrical conduit fittings. The men wanted to complete the job before the end of the shift. I rushed up the stairs, but when I neared the top I had to grip the handrail hard. I was losing my balance and felt as if I were about to free-fall out of my body. It was an unsettling sensation, but it passed, and I continued on my assignment, refusing to worry about it.

A few days after that experience, I began to feel burning sensations in my right leg. My right hand went numb. The feeling in my hand returned within five days, but the burning sensations became more frequent and felt as if a blowtorch were ravaging my body, starting in the middle of my lower back, traveling to the right and slowly working its way down my leg. The heat intensified at my knee and continued down my leg. I felt as if flames were bursting through my toes. The pain was almost unbearable.

The following week, while I was studying for a final exam, I felt a strange movement across my chest and felt something race down both arms and they went numb at the same time. Although I was scared and feared the worst, I tried not to alarm my family. I mentioned it casually at work the next day. Some thought that, perhaps, I had pinched a nerve. I visited an ear, nose, and throat specialist whom I had been seeing for other problems. He suggested that I visit a neurologist. I made an appointment and waited.

While I waited, the burning sensations in my legs grew more severe. Both legs were on fire but the sensation was more severe in my right leg. Sometimes I would recover from one attack and immediately experience another. My legs cramped, and walking became difficult. I couldn't wait for my scheduled appointment, so I called back for another referral and was able to get one a month earlier. I met Dr. Goldin during the latter part of 1995. Over a period of three months, he sent me for an MRI and conducted other tests.

One test, an Electromyograph (EMG), was crucial for a diagnosis of MS. Needle electrodes were inserted into muscles in my legs and arms, and small amps of current were delivered to the nerves, one lead at a time. I think I had at least 8 electrodes inserted at once. It felt as if 20 amps of current were passing through the leads, and I flopped around on the table like a fish out of water. Next, a long needle was inserted into some of my muscles to gauge their reaction. After the test, I lay sprawled on the table for quite a while until I regained enough composure to leave. It was extremely painful, and I lost a lot of blood from the wounds made by the needles. I felt awful, although I later understood why the test had to be administered. It helped to assess nerve damage. Dr. Goldin prescribed medication for the burning sensations in my legs.

About a week later, while I was at work, Dr. Goldin reached my husband at home, just before he left for work, and asked him to have me call. My husband paged me, and when I reached him he told me to call the doctor. I called from the phone in my work area, with the other electricians listening to a one-sided conversation. When I replaced the receiver in its cradle, everyone wanted to know what the doctor had said. They all looked so concerned for me, I felt I had to break the tension.

Another apprentice asked, "What did the doctor say?

I replied, "He said I have an abnormal brain."

They all laughed and said, "We could have told him that."

Actually, the doctor had said, "You have abnormalities of the brain."

A few nights later, I was sitting at home when Dr. Goldin called. He wanted to know if I had been in an accident because the MRI had revealed a spot on my spinal cord. He had mentioned to me in earlier exams that MS was among the possible causes for my symptoms (as was a pinched nerve). He wanted me to see a neurosurgeon and also wanted to perform a lumbar puncture.

I visited the neurosurgeon first. He examined me and looked at the results of my MRI scan.

He told me, "You have UBOs of the brain."

"I have what?"

"Have you heard of UFOs?"

"Yes, of course."

"UBOs are Unidentified Bright Objects. You have them all over your brain," he said, smiling compassionately. I learned that these UBOs, also known as "small T2 hyperintensities," were lesions. Depending on where UBOs are located, their presence on an MRI can be helpful in confirming a diagnosis of MS.

Later Dr. Goldin performed the spinal tap, a procedure involving penetrating my spinal cord with a needle. He concentrated on inserting the needle into my spinal cord, and I didn't want him to miss. He asked me to see him after the testing. It was December 15, 1995, a day I'll never forget. I left work, hurried home, showered, grabbed my schoolbooks, and rushed to Dr. Goldin's office. He looked at me and said, "I don't know how to tell you this, so I'm just going to say it. You have Multiple Sclerosis." I glanced up at him and said, "Please hold that thought. I have two final exams to take tonight. It's important to me that I take them."

My worst nightmare had come true, but I didn't have time to break down. I'd come too far to quit. I left Dr. Goldin's office and raced to school. While taking my first final, I felt an explosion in my head. My mind went blank and I forgot everything I had learned. I talked myself out of the terror that was rising within me. I slowly looked at all the questions on the exam and answered what came easily. As my anxiety subsided, the knowledge began to return. I was able to finish my final exams and passed all of my classes. I was now free to begin to deal with MS. It was clear that MS wanted to deal with me.

A few days after my visit with Dr. Goldin, I was traveling on the expressway with my daughter, who was then ten years old. As I neared home, the car in front of me suddenly became two. I knew I needed to stay calm and to exit the expressway safely. Glancing to my left and seeing just one lane, I knew that at least I still had peripheral vision. I was able to drive the short distance home.

We flew to Florida to visit family for Christmas. I experienced double vision the entire time. My eyes would dart around like jumping beans. During January of 1996, numbness began to spread through my body, and my brain wasn't functioning properly. I knew I should have a clearer perception of events, but my thought processes had become jumbled. Considering the prognosis for people afflicted with Multiple Sclerosis, I feared for my family, my job, and myself.

Dr. Goldin prescribed IV steroids over a period of seven days. They helped to restore my ability to function more normally. I began to accept the fact I had a debilitating disease that strikes without warning. There is no cure for MS, and the disease does terrible things to the body. During this time, Dr. Jack Kevorkian was popular for his stance on assisted suicides. I learned that approximately one-third of the people Dr. Kevorkian assisted with suicide had MS. Being newly diagnosed with MS, the knowledge that people with my disease often resort to suicide did nothing to comfort me.

One day I needed to wash clothes and carefully descended to the basement. As I tried to return upstairs, I found I couldn't lift either leg. I sat down on the steps to figure out a game plan. The solution hit me. I pushed myself up, backwards, step by step until I reached the top, avoiding the need to lift my legs. When I reached the top of the stairs, I spun my body around, pushed up with my hands from the floor, grabbed the handrail with one hand and pulled myself up.

After five weeks, I was able to return to work from my sick leave. I knew the men I worked with would support me, and with the support of my managers, I would be okay. I was right. The employees at American Axle rallied behind me.

In May of 1996, I helped chaperone my daughter's fifth grade trip to Cedar Point, a popular amusement park in Ohio. A group of mothers and a father, two Jews, one Catholic, one Seventh Day Adventist, one Baptist, and one Black, comprised my group of chaperones. We spoke about all the taboo subjects, such as religion, politics, and O.J. Simpson. We learned some interesting facts about one another. We learned that were all humans and Americans.

When we arrived at the park, my group made its way to the Blue Streak roller coaster, the first roller coaster I had ever ridden. I remembered it very well. The young girls I chaperoned wanted me to ride with them and, against my better judgment, I let them persuade me. The young girl who rode with me wanted me to put my arm around her to hold her. The safety bar came down and locked us in place. As soon as we took off and ascended to the first big drop, I felt a strange fluttering sensation running down my left arm, and suddenly it was paralyzed. Here I was, riding a roller coaster with a dead arm. I looped my right arm around the safety bar and began to pray that it would maintain its mobility. It was the ride of my life.

Fortunately, the young girl had no knowledge of my predicament. I slid my body into hers, attempting to comfort her as I prayed for this ride to end without me flying out of the car. When we left the ride after my terrifying ordeal, my daughter asked what was wrong with my arm. I told her it had just fallen asleep. A few hours passed before it returned to normal. I had minor incidents with the MS after that, but nothing I found hard to handle until a year later, in March, when the feeling that someone was using a blowtorch inside my legs began again.

I made an appointment with Dr. Goldin. I had believed that the medicine he prescribed previously had taken care of the problem. I would learn that relapsing-remitting MS, the type that affects me, is characterized by an increase or worsening of symptoms, called a relapse or an exacerbation, followed by a period of remission, during which symptoms may disappear or lessen significantly. MS symptoms vary from one person to another, so the course of the disease is somewhat unpredictable. All I knew was that the medication for the burning pain in my legs didn't work. Only time makes them go away. This MS flare up had ended. I continued to work in pain while I waited for my doctor's appointment.

After Dr. Goldin examined me, he turned his back and walked away, shaking his head. I remember watching him and thinking, why is he shaking his head? He informed me that I was experiencing an exacerbation of the MS and asked me if I wanted to try riding it out or try IV steroids. I knew steroids were harsh on the body and should only be used as a last resort, so I agreed to try riding it out. I had been through the burns before and didn't imagine they could get any worse. I was so wrong. This exacerbation brought a new degree of pain with leg burns and severe cramping. I tried to be brave and tough it out, but I couldn't stand the unremitting pain.

On Good Friday, March 1997, while I was working in Plant 1, the fiery sensation traveled down my right leg, and then my left. A new production supervisor happened to walk past me while this was happening. When he saw me grimace, he came over to help me. He was young and scared. Through clenched teeth, I told him that this exacerbation just had to run its course. My ordeal probably aged him 10 years on the spot, but he stayed with me. As soon as I was able to return to my work site, I told my partner, Colin, I'd be right back, and went to call Dr. Goldin. I knew at that point that I would never try to ride out the leg burns again. When he answered, I only had two words to utter: "Monday, steroids."

I was admitted to the hospital the day after Easter for seven days of intravenous steroid treatments. I refused to allow my young daughter to see me hooked up to the IV because I didn't want to frighten her. I waited until she went home to have my drug of choice, steroids. As the drug flowed through my veins, I remember feeling like a junkie waiting for the sweet relief I expected it to bring. It came that night and a feeling of exhaustion washed over my body. I was so tired from all the pain. The effect was dramatic. The next morning I was able to concentrate on my homework. During my hospital stay, I kept up with my schoolwork.

My husband came to see me one night to show me some mail he had received. It was a funny card from my coworkers. They were sympathizing with him because I was going to be home all day for a while. I appreciated their support. The men at American Axle were great men, and I felt so blessed. While in the hospital, I knew the fibroid tumors were growing, but I tried not to think about it. Released from the hospital the following Monday morning, I was back in school that evening. Most people were amazed that I'd returned, but I was determined to accomplish my goal. Thanks to the supportive people I was working with at the time, I knew I'd be okay.

After three weeks I was able to return to work. When I did, I noticed that a picture of my daughter that I kept at my workstation was missing. A few weeks later, it resurfaced. My friend, Roy, had taken it, and his wife had my daughter's face placed on a dollar bill. Roy and I had a great relationship. He was our strongman and no one bothered him, except me. It was a mutual picking on each other. Once, when I was working on the railroad tracks in the rain, dripping wet, Roy pulled up alongside on an in-plant vehicle. He patted the passenger seat and told me, "It's nice and dry in here." Another time the journeymen were having their daily morning meeting to discuss the day's work. Roy's back was to me. I stood in the aisle pitching pennies at him as the other journeyman laughed. One penny landed on top of his head. He jumped up with his fist clenched, ready to knock someone out but I was in the aisle, safely away from him. He told me, "You're crazy." I responded, "Takes one to know one." I loved Roy as a person.

When I left American Axle Roy bought me a guardian angel. He said the angel would look over me since he couldn't. His wife took it to Mass and had it blessed. Another day during the morning meeting Roy barked at me, "Camille, get me some coffee." In my sweetest voice I said, "Sure Roy. What do you want in it?" "Cream and sugar" he bellowed. I took off to get his coffee, but then I heard him yell, "Camille." I returned to him. "Yes," I said looking very angelic. "Forget it. I wouldn't trust anything you bring me to drink." He was absolutely right. He hadn't specified how much cream and sugar, so I was going to load his coffee with sugar and cream. These exchanges had nothing to do with my race or sex.

One time, Roy sent me to get an open-end crescent wrench from his toolbox.

I was on my way when he yelled, "Camille!"

"Yes, Roy."

"Don't bother my gun in my toolbox."

I moved his gun to the side and grabbed the wrench. We worked in a very dangerous neighborhood and some people carried guns for safety. I knew several people who did, and once witnessed police chasing a suspect with their guns drawn from the lunchroom window of the plant.

One night I had my hair done at a salon. It was very late when we finished. My hairdresser had already taken off when I inserted my key into the ignition of my car. Suddenly, I felt another strange sensation. It was as if a huge body builder was standing behind me with his hands on my shoulders, pinning me down. Then it felt as if his friend, "the Incredible Hulk," was ripping my arm out of its socket. My left arm was paralyzed. Here I was, sitting alone in an almost pitch-black strip mall, with a useless arm; the perfect victim for a predator. I was terrified, but needed to try to get out of panic mode and find a way out of the situation. The steering column on my car had to be unlocked with my left hand, but my arm refused to cooperate with my brain. I began to pray. I couldn't even lift my hand, but I managed to use my knees to unlock the steering column. I drove home with a paralyzed arm.

MS was affecting my tear ducts, making me to appear to be crying. One day at work, Colin saw me and asked what was wrong. For some reason, the expression of concern on his face made me laugh. The more I laughed, the harder I cried. We were scheduled to work in the air that day and I was scaring him. He was leery of working in the manlift with me. Not knowing much about Multiple Sclerosis, he probably thought I might flip out. The thought of this made me laugh and cry even harder. Finally he understood that I was able to work and would explain it to him after the tears stopped. Humor often helped me deal with my illness, and I'm thankful to have been gifted with a good sense of humor.

CHAPTER 4

On Nov 14, 1996, I attained my goal of becoming a journey-man. By then I had been working for GM almost 20 years. I had persevered and was pleased with myself for not having succumbed to defeat. Randy, an electrician in Plant 6, bought me a cake, and all the men congratulated and celebrated with me. I returned to the construction gang, which I loved. There was so much to learn. I loved bending pipe, running conduit, pulling wire harnesses, wiring machines, building new panel boxes, hanging lights, installing circuit breakers, driving manlifts, and working in the switch houses. Many GM tradesmen were leaving American Axle in order to flow back to GM. New journeymen were hired to replace the GM returnees. Most of them came through the construction gang first. For some, it was their first time working with a woman. My electrical leader wanted them to get used to working with females, and I often had the lead position because I knew the plant.

Even so, as soon as I became a journeyman, I immediately submitted an "area hire" form. Although I loved the Gear employees, I had too many years at GM to stay. I had high seniority there, but the company was not sure to last. (In fact, American Axle closed the plant early 2012.) I put in a transfer request to the Romulus Engine plant in Romulus, MI. Quite a few of the men who trained me had transferred there.

I also heard that Pontiac Truck was looking for electricians for their new 800 series, which included the Chevy Silverado and the GMC Sierra. It was located 11 miles from my house and would be the third GM facility I worked. I applied for the job and I received a call the following week giving me a date in May to report to Pontiac. Pontiac Truck had called me before Romulus engine. I left the good people at American Axle to go to Pontiac to work with cheaters, drunks and drug addicts.

My supervisor asked me, "Do you really want to leave us?"

"No. I have to leave because I have over 20 years' seniority with GM."

"We don't want to see you leave, but we understand why you must."

After working at the Gear & Axle, I was ill-prepared for what was awaiting me in Pontiac: a corrupt union, sexual harassment, gender and race discrimination, and bullying by GM management. It was 1997, and Pontiac East Assembly was on an 87-day strike, which delayed my report date. Union officials were accused of supporting an illegal strike. It took ten years to bring these union officials to justice in the courts. In June, 2007, two union representatives, Donny Douglas and Jay Campbell, were convicted of extorting General Motors and violating the Labor-Management Relations Act when they threatened to prolong the strike unless the company hired their unqualified friends and family members. A third man, Bill Coffey, died before trial. All three were bargainers for the local contract. Donny Douglas was a UAW International rep. I had communicated with both Coffey and Douglas, begging for their help to make management stop harassing me and live up to their contract agreements. I also spoke about the sexual harassment directed at me. Donny Douglas, not a pleasant man to deal with, he seemed determined to protect the guys committing fraud against General Motors. He seemed angry at me for exposing it, but the management was fully aware at that plant.

Bill Coffey had been my committee man. I had spoken with him several times about the men bullying me and about the supervisor's decision that I would work seven days a week, to no avail. This union would not help a qualified Black female journeyman electrician, but they committed extortion to get their unqualified friends and relatives hired as skilled tradesmen. The union fought for jobs for unqualified White males, but helped the company harass a fully qualified Black female who had passed the test on her own. And then they took the plant out on an illegal strike.

A Michigan judge at first tried to mitigate the charges and then threw them out. The Federal Department of Justice picked up the case and convicted Douglas and Campbell. If the company was experiencing extortion from the union, it was their duty to report it to the FBI. Instead, the managers at Pontiac Truck went along with it.

I knew four other electricians reporting to work in Pontiac. I had worked with them at American Axle and we had good relationships, so I did not feel isolated. Some other tradesmen were transferring from American Axle to Pontiac, and I knew all of them also. The strike ended and our new report date to Pontiac Truck became July 28, 1997.

My decision to accept the Pontiac job was one I would soon regret. The place was a living nightmare. Pontiac Local 594 was the worst local I have ever experienced. It was as if I had waded into the pits of hell. UAW seemed to stand for "United Against Workers" or "United Against Women." The "good ol' boys" were horrible, and so were the Black males. The Black men at American Axle had done everything they could to support me and teach me. The Black men in Pontiac did everything they could to tear me down and put me in my place.

The first morning, after passing through the medical department for our physicals, we who were transferred skilled tradesmen were swept away to a classroom for various bits of information and some aspects of training. At the end of the shift, the superintendent of maintenance, Jack Tolbin, welcomed us. It was clear from his arrogant stance that he believed he was the King and we were entering his kingdom. He had been previously employed at a brewery. When that job ended, he came to Pontiac East Assembly as an electrician. Many of the electricians in the body shop also came from the brewery and were good friends of Jack's. In his 12 years in the same department he was promoted from supervisor to superintendent. I had never seen a superintendent promoted after working their whole time at GM in the same department. Much of the terror I experienced there could have been prevented if the superintendent had not been such good friends with these male electricians. It was obvious that his allegiance was to his old friends and that he could not effectively manage them.

The following morning we received our new job assignments. Mine was to an area called "Car Trac." The cab of the truck, where the driver and passengers sit, is assembled through Car Trac. I had never worked with robots, and needed training. When I reported to Pontiac, they were nearing the end of their "400 Project," which is what the old model trucks were called. I was hired for the new "GMT 800 Project," and eventually received the proper training.

There were six electricians in my new area. Two were originally hired in the plant, three were from area hire, and the last was a new hire. Area hire employees come from other plants. The others were that were originally hired in this plant considered this their "home plant." I was the only woman and the only Black in Car Trac. The first thing that struck me as odd was that the robots were not enclosed in a fenced off area. There was dull yellow paint marking their envelopes or their range of motion, which are the danger areas around a robot, but nothing to protect a worker from inadvertently entering their path. The envelopes should cover the full path of the robots. If you didn't know about robots and their envelopes, you would be unaware of the lurking danger.

We each received a hammer and a crescent wrench and were instructed by the production supervisor to change welding caps. We didn't know what changing welding caps meant. A seasoned electrician showed us how to change them. Getting close to robots that were active was very dangerous. They moved unexpectedly, and we were forbidden to cut off power to them. At American Axle we were taught to go to zero energy, which means pulling the disconnect. In Pontiac, the supervisors were angry if the electricians did this. Keep in mind that many of the supervisors in Pontiac had no trade experience. Management could have gone to the restaurant across the street and hired the cook, who would have been just as knowledgeable about the skilled trades as the supervisors for whom I had to work.

As often happens, one day a robot crashed into a cab, and it was necessary for a trained electrician to carefully ease the robot out of the crash and return it to its home position. One of the trained, seasoned electricians convinced the supervisor to instruct a newly hired electrician to do this. The new man, like the rest of us, had never been trained to use the control unit for the robot. Instead of ensuring that the job was performed quickly and effectively by an electrician with experience, the supervisor insisted that the untrained electrician do the assignment. The result was predictable. It only created more down time and the possibility of more equipment damage. There were two men in the supervisor's department who knew the job, but he seemed scared to order them to do it.

In this work environment, men were constantly screaming obscenities at each other and at the supervisors. I had never experienced this to such a degree at any of the previous facilities where I'd worked. It seemed the supervisors worked through the path of least resistance, which usually meant the new hire and me. Supervisors were safe in their assumption that I would not use filthy language on them.

Most of the supervisors were unskilled and had only limited knowledge of what they were asking the Skilled Trades to do. One supervisor ordered me to cut the live 480 volts at an electrical conduit fitting called an "LB." I would definitely *not* consider cutting live 480 volts at the LB without accessing the power bus and de-energizing it. This supervisor displayed total ignorance of what he was asking me to do. Thank goodness I knew better or I might be dead now.

At that time the management had a rule that you had to do what any manager told you to do. If, en route to do one job, you were stopped by another supervisor, you were expected to drop what the previous one had said and do what the new one told you. It's a wonder anything was ever completed. No one kept track of what was happening. It was a dysfunctional, chaotic system, and nothing but a power play by the supervision. As far as the work actually being completed, no one seemed to care. I had never been around such sorry supervision in all my time in the plants. "Supervisor" was a misnomer. They had no idea how to supervise.

One day all of the guys in the crib, which is the area where we sat in while waiting on a job, cursed out a supervisor for his incompetence. From then on, he avoided contact with them. Any time he entered the crib to summon an electrician, he would look at me and call me forward with the flick of his finger. He didn't dare say anything to the men. Out of frustration, I finally asked, "You have six electricians in the crib, why don't you get one of the guys to work?"

He answered, "Shut up, and do as I tell you. Don't worry about the guys."

Another production supervisor, Carlo O'Toole, wanted me to hang welding cables on racks. The cables were extremely heavy and required two people to manipulate them. There were five of us in the crib. Carlo walked into the crib and chose me. As I accompanied him to the job site, he explained what he wanted me to do.

"The cables are heavy," he said. "Go get one of the guys to help you."

I told him it was his job to distribute the work, and it would be up to him to order another hourly employee to work. Although he knew the cables were heavy and needed two people, he didn't want to challenge a man; so he tried to get me to do his job. He wanted me to use my "feminine wiles" to get the guys to assist me. Of course, then I would have experienced even more harassment.

I said, "I'll get the ladder. You get the employee." When I returned with the ladder, I saw that instead of getting one of the guys sitting in the crib, he'd assigned the newly hired electrician, who was already on a job, to work with me. Somehow, I was not surprised.

We new skilled tradesmen at this plant received minimal robot safety training. I was instructed by a seasoned electrician not to pull the robot disconnect, but to turn off the robot's water. The robot should not be able to run without the water. Astonished, I asked him, "Why don't you want me to pull the power disconnect, which is proper lockout procedure?"

"If you disable the water, the robot's water saver signal should fault and disable the robot from moving. Don't pull the disconnect or the supervisor will be angry."

"What about my safety?"

The electrician shrugged his shoulders and walked away.

I was nearing a robot to change caps, but I had an uncomfortable feeling. The fine hairs on my arms were standing up. I disabled the water, but didn't immediately approach the robot. I stood back and observed. The next cab came in for welding, and I watched as one of my worst fears played out before my eyes. The robot took off without water and began to weld. The water safety switch had failed. If I had been standing where I normally stood to change caps, this robot would have smashed me square in the face. I stood there in shock. There is no doubt in my mind that I could have been seriously injured, killed, or maimed for life. GM would more than likely have accused my dead body of not following safety procedures because I didn't pull the disconnect switch to stop the robot from moving. It was a frightening time in the body shop.

In another situation I can't forget, a general foreman wanted an electrical shunt replaced on a robot gun. The cabs would stop at various stations for welding. When released, a new cab would approach to be welded. The robot repair position did not leave enough clearance for a person to work safely while the line was moving, and so this general foreman stood nearby and yelled for me to duck when a new cab was approaching. Although there were plenty of experienced people to do the job, he chose me; and he wanted to keep the line moving while I worked, jeopardizing my safety. He placed me in the dangerous situation of having to pull my head back every time a new cab approached. The metal on the cab was sharp enough to split my head open if I had been struck. It was as if my life was expendable.

This general foreman soon afterwards transferred to another plant. Word circulated throughout the body shop that the transfer was due to a "noose" incident involving a young, Black, female, salaried employee. Rumor had it that he took a Black female doll, tied a rope around its neck, and had the doll hanging in his office. When he called her into his office, she saw the hanging doll. He laughed when he saw the horrified expression on her face.

I had never been in a plant where general foremen and superintendents would bypass protocol and address employees any time they felt like it. There have always been chains of command. For most people, being addressed by a superintendent would immediately be intimidating because of the power a superintendent wields. General foremen had the authority to decide who was fired and what job a worker would receive. They were in control of the foreman. At my previous facilities, employees had an immediate foreman to whom they reported. Here the superintendents and general foremen were doing the jobs of production supervisors. I always wondered what their jobs were, since they found so much time to micromanage. I had also never seen so many high level managers in one department. This place was a hideout for an overabundance of white collar employees with not enough to do.

Equipment training courses were scheduled for the electricians working on the new GMT 800 Project building the Silverado and Sierra Trucks. The two shifts not in training worked twelve hour shifts, Monday through Friday, to cover production. We also worked weekends. Carlo, the production supervisor, told me to work all of the Saturdays and all of the Sundays. I balked. I'd noticed that he didn't order the male employees to work any Sundays. I called my union steward, and asked him to speak with the superintendent about this. I explained to my union steward that I had MS and that, until I could adjust to working long hours, I didn't want to work twelve hours on Sundays. I understood about covering production during the week, and didn't want to allow any of my medical problems to interfere with my work due to my lack of rest. I was already working 62 ½ hours per week, Monday through Friday, to cover production and 12 1/2 hours on weekends.

My union rep, Bill Coffey, returned a few days later from the committee office and told me he had spoken with the superintendent and that everything was okay. Working every Sunday was not in our contract. Sundays were voluntary. I worked some Sundays but, because fatigue is a major problem for people afflicted with MS, I took care not to exhaust myself. My previous union training had taught me well to try to work the situation out before it was out of control.

CHAPTER 5

I knew the fibroid tumors were growing from the physical changes I was experiencing, but I didn't want to miss the months of training that were scheduled to begin in January, 1998. I knew I needed surgery, and also a new doctor. In December of 1997, I met Dr. Joseph Berenholz. My referral nurse had respect and admiration for him. I appreciated his professionalism, and knew after a few minutes of talking with him that I wanted him to perform my hysterectomy.

During the exam, I saw the expression on his face.

I said to him, "Big, aren't they?"

After the exam, he explained that one tumor was the size of a cantaloupe, another a little smaller, and another the size of a baseball. He told me to let him know when I wanted him to take care of the problem. Since my classes began in January, I scheduled the surgery for February 3, 1998. I would have six to eight weeks to recuperate at home before my next round of classes. The day of my surgery one question kept replaying in my mind. My grandmother died of ovarian cancer, so I asked Dr. Berenholz, "When does a woman normally know when she has ovarian cancer?"

He replied, "When it is too late."

I spent the next two months recuperating. Three weeks after the surgery GM called me and informed me that they were looking for a job I could do so that I could return to work. I was lying there, still in pain. The stitches in my sliced-open abdomen had not healed. When I moved it felt as if my guts would spill out on the floor. Because the wound was subject to reopening, I couldn't wear anything pressing on it, and here was GM Pontiac searching for a job for me, three weeks after major surgery! I sensed something strange in the air then, and wondered why they would place my life and health at risk. This plant was so bad I began to fear that one of the guys would deliberately hit me in the abdomen and claim it was an accident if I had returned early. Imagine, three weeks off work after a total hysterectomy.

I returned to work on March 30, 1998. My eyes were finally opened wide, and I took a good look at the new world I'd ventured into. I was appalled. This place was loaded with all sorts of discrimination. For example, GM did not stop a sanitation worker from riding all over the plant, on a plant vehicle, wearing shirts, hats, and scarves emblazoned with the Confederate emblem. There are cultural clashes, and the man had a right to his own beliefs; but GM should have barred him from wearing this symbol of intolerance and hatred on their property. Allowing him to wear it contributed to what is known as a "hostile work environment."

When I returned to my department, I immediately put in a shift preference for the third shift. The day shift, from 6:30 a.m. to 3:00 p.m., was a favorite. Second shift was from 2:30 p.m. to 11 p.m., and third shift was from 10:30 p.m. to 7 a.m. Bumping is the method of moving from shift to shift by seniority. Another electrician had bumped to the first shift from the second shift, and the first shift had not sent his replacement to the second shift. Since I had still been on medical leave, I was not on the payroll the preceding Wednesday, and so was not eligible to be bumped. The superintendent, Miles, explained that although it was management's mistake, I would have to pay for their negligence and report to afternoons. I could put in a shift preference a week later. They had sent the guy who was suppose to go on second shift to the third shift. It was their way of protecting him from second shift.This eligibility for bumps was in our local contract. I did not think this was fair, and called for my union steward. Why should I suffer the penalty for management's incompetence? This management was incapable of making a simple shift change.

My union steward actually helped me this time. I reported to the third shift. Little did I realize that my taking a stand would be taken personally by the management, and I would pay dearly for it later.

I was assigned to a construction job two weeks after I returned to work. This management team assigned all the transplanted electricians, those of us who have worked at other GM facilities, to this job. The work required running pipe and wires to a new machine. Our transplanted electricians were extremely qualified individuals; and yet, not one electrician originally from the Pontiac location was on assignment for this job. I had no objection to construction jobs because I had the experience. The problem was, I had barely recuperated from a total hysterectomy, which everyone was well aware of. This management had immediately assigned me to a job that placed maximum stress on my incision.

The other female electrician, a woman who was called "the Queen," never received job assignments like this. She was a White female, and management gave her preferential treatment. She stayed in the manager's office. She would report to work and head directly there to sit with the supervisors all day. I did the job, but it was extremely hard on my abdomen, which I believe delayed my healing. The GM supervisor, Cecil, called me aside to ask me if I could still achieve an orgasm after the surgery. I looked at him, shook my head and walked away. I couldn't believe that a GM supervisor was asking me personal sexual questions. Derek had approached me to ask if I had a hanging stomach. "Ugh, Camille," he said.

"Like you would ever see it," I snapped. "Get your ignorant behind away from me."

It was no surprise me that I later sprained my ankle slipping on oil, and after had to fight to get the proper medical attention. I was sent back to my department with light duty instructions by GM's medical doctor, but this management didn't care. They forced me to maintain the line, entering slippery work areas covered in weld slag. I was in pain from my sprained ankle and the chances of my falling were increased. If I got hurt, so what? Big deal.

We continued to work twelve hours for training purposes as I continued to have problems with my MS. There was nothing too severe until May, 1998, when I began to feel strange sensations running through my body. I was also not seeing well with my right eye. Everything looked like a mirage in electrical panel grey. I was afraid that I was going blind. I called my neurologist, who put me through a battery of eye exams. It was another exacerbation of my MS, and this time the symptom was optic neuritis. My right eye was almost blind. The doctor felt at this point it was too late to take steroids, so I had no choice but to ride it out. At this time I learned that there was a chance it might spread to my left eye. I tried not to complain and continued to work every day, while the management was fully aware of my challenged vision. I had told the managers I was having problems seeing. The Medical department had my medical records.

We were still taking classes, but I was finding it difficult to see the computer monitor. All the beautiful, bright colors of the body shop, orange, red, yellow, and blue, were dimmed. Throughout all the misery I was experiencing with MS, my friend, Dirk, told me this was the first time he actually saw me scared; and he was right. I was terrified. Over the course of the next four months, my eyesight began to return; but another surprise awaited me. The optic neuritis had spread to my left eye. I remember sitting on the back porch by myself, praying not to lose my eyesight. My prayers were answered when the vision in my left eye returned within two months. I have permanent nerve damage to my right eye, and under stressful situations, the tingling sensation in my body increases and I experience blurred vision. But I'm overjoyed to be able to see.

In August 1998, production moved to the new Body Shop. Our training completed, it was time to use what we had learned. On the first night of start-up for the new 800 Project, I was working in an area known as B-Zone, the place where the assembly line begins. I was the least experienced journeyman there. After working in the old body shop for 12 years, the guys originally from this plant were used to working with this type of equipment. I had never worked in a body shop. I knew I would learn, but start-up night was not a good night for me to fly solo.

The maintenance management team had about four maintenance supervisors that night and most of them were telling me what to do. They made me maintain two lines at the same time, and because my line was the beginning of the truck, the other supervisors lines were not running. If the other lines were not running, then there were many electricians doing nothing, and they should have been sent to help me. The work to which I was assigned involved producing floor pans, the bottom of the truck where your feet rest. When finished, they were to have carpet and floor mats installed. I asked the managers to get one of the guys who was sleeping to help, but it seemed to me they were scared to ask because they didn't dispatch anyone. Over thirty electricians, and only three or four were working! Some of the electricians had gone to the bar and some had gone home. There was supposed to be another electrician on the second line, but he had disappeared from the area. No one knew where he had gone; nor did they care. They all had friends to punch their time clocks. While no action was taken against the electrician for his disappearance, the management continued to put pressure on me, with threats of discipline, to keep the lines going by myself. I was able to keep both assembly lines running, but I was exhausted.

It was 3 a.m. and I had been working all night while guys slept around me. A supervisor whom I did not know, Shane, approached me. He said, "I hate to do this, but I need you to go to another area and change the motor on the MIG welder."

At that time I had no idea what a MIG welder was, just that it was used to weld the hinges to the doors. MIG stands for "metal inert gas." It's a type of gas metal arc welding (GMAW). The welder is fed automatically from a huge spool of wire. There were two men assigned to that area.

Why didn't they change their own motors? Supervisor Shane said, "I will get you help, but you will change that motor." He ventured to the other end of the body shop to get another Black electrician. This electrician worked on the boxcar line making truck beds. His department was the only other line running. On that shift, out of approximately 35 electricians, only three were Black. This management made sure to keep two of us constantly working. We changed the motor.

Where were the men who worked on that line while we changed the motor? Both had disappeared from their assigned work area. One had gone home, and the other had gone to the bar and then home. I would later learn that they were the "untouchables." Both were among my future tormentors.

I wanted to further my education and study electrical engineering. I needed two classes to complete my Associate's Degree and asked a couple of the guys if they would they trade shifts with me until I finished school if I was bumped to another shift. My two friends from American Axle said, "No problem. We'll help you." When I approached the superintendent, Heath, and spoke with him about it, he said, "Go ahead and register. If something occurs, I'll hold you for 45 days so you can complete your schooling." Heath was a transplanted manager. He did not originate from Pontiac Truck, but had worked at several facilities before arriving at Pontiac. I believe he was as shocked at the conditions at Pontiac as I was.

I registered for my classes. The night before I was to start, a supervisor came to tell me that if I were bumped, I would have to transfer to the new shift. The superintendent with whom I had won the "shift battle" and another who also had no desire to help me further my education had overridden Heath. They didn't want me to have more knowledge than the Queen. Heath knew what the other two members of management had decided and was so upset that he couldn't speak to me. I said, "Thank you, Heath, for at least trying to treat me fairly. I know this isn't your fault." All he could do was nod his head, obviously thankful that I understood. It seems that when I won the battle over the shift change after returning from medical leave, the supervisors had taken it personally. Committee calls normally were not taken so personally. Supervisors usually didn't have such thin skin. It was different here. I felt as if I was working with children.

Although the management knew who slipped out of work and who used drugs and alcohol on the job, they continued to allow this type of behavior. These same employees, protected by this management, arrived at work inebriated or stoned on drugs without any manager challenging them. Management also used alcohol on the job. One supervisor in particular reported to work almost every night reeking of alcohol. The employees remaining on the job were expected to cover the missing employees who were defrauding the company.

Our superintendent of maintenance, Jack Tolbin, had became a supervisor and was promoted to superintendent without ever leaving the body shop and not having gained any exposure to GM's different styles of management. I had worked in two previous GM facilities and had never seen internal promotions like this. Jack set up his personal kingdom inside the GM infrastructure. The UAW/GM Contract seemed to mean nothing to him. His friends could pretty much do anything they wanted without facing discipline. At the same time, I was always at work and always forced to cover for other electricians when they refused to do their jobs.

I came to understand that the features of Jack's kingdom were corruption, drugs, alcohol, sexual harassment, violence, fraud, assault, discrimination against people with disabilities, and discrimination against women. His subjects, GM managers, seemed to go to any length to force me to bow down to him as if he were a god, just as they did. As time went by, I realized that most of the managers I met seemed to be interested mainly in trying to get promoted to the next level. Unfortunately, they seemed to have a callous attitude towards the quality of the products and safety laws to me.

In September 1998, I was bumped to the first shift. Reporting to work in the door areas, where the truck doors were built. Although each line had an electrician assigned to it, I was again forced to maintain two lines by myself. We had to be on top of the breakdowns to avoid costly downtime. I needed and asked for help for two weeks, and received none. The male electrician was on vacation. He was responsible for the left door line and I was responsible for the right. The lines were across from each other. We were considered partners because we each had a door line, but we did not work the lines together. He was responsible for his line and I for mine. There were vacation replacement electricians available, but management chose not to replace my partner. The result was unnecessary downtime.

When Roland returned from his unapproved vacation, things didn't change much. Because of his gruff personality, other employees and supervisors were afraid of him; and so, I was summoned for all the calls on both lines. The production workers would place their maintenance call lights on, and he would not respond, so they would alert me that his line was down. He was on his line, reading books and ignoring the calls, the sounding alarms, and the flashing marquee. I had to respond to the breakdown on my partner's line or I would face discipline.

The work distribution should have been even, but it never was. On weekends the supervisors assigned the majority of the work to me. One of my future partners was my supervisor at the time. Corky piled work on me while he gave Roland one job, that of assisting the machine repairmen. Roland's work totaled approximately a half hour. I was walking back to my area to gather some tools to complete my assignment when Corky stopped me. As he was speaking to me, the machine repairmen finished their job on Roland's line. Corky glanced at Roland and then told me. "Someone needs to change caps and reset the steppers."

I said "I am currently on a job. Why don't you tell Roland? You gave him this assignment, and he's just sitting there looking at you. It's his line and his responsibility."

"Well, someone needs to change tips," he said as he walked quickly away. This supervisor had previously worked with my partner and it was evident he was afraid of him.

My partner didn't report to work for a couple of days. A supervisor, Mitch, was running around in a panic trying to figure out why he had not shown up. Finally Mitch came around and told me, "You have to run both lines. Roland is on an unapproved vacation. You will keep both lines running or I'll discipline you." After Roland returned to work, he faced no discipline for his action.

One day I was sitting in my area with a few of the other electricians. Suddenly, a wrapped condom flew into the area. A supervisor had thrown it. I confronted him and said, "I work with all men and do not appreciate your implication. I am going to Labor Relations with this condom."

My threat produced an arrogant laugh from him. He had no fear of Labor and said, "Go ahead, I'll escort you there." What did I expect from a man who would come to work and discuss with the male tradesmen his sexual intimacies with his wife? He was a disgusting creature. Instead of checking to see if I was being sexually harassed, the supervisor was throwing condoms my way. These kinds of situations continued until I was bumped to the third shift. I ended up in the same area but on the opposite line.

Henry was a production worker and, as he proclaimed to all, a Christian minister. He was a large man, and thought I should hop to his tune. All night long he played religious radio programs so loudly I couldn't hear myself think. I asked him kindly to lower the volume because we had to "share the air." He responded by turning it up.

I approached him and said, "Henry, I have nothing against religion, but I don't want to listen to a minister screaming and hollering all night. This does nothing for my spirit."

Henry looked at me with his big, dark eyes. "You know you are supposed to defer to me. You're a woman."

I stared back in disbelief. "I am not your wife and you are not my husband. Your religion may teach you that women should be subservient to you, but this is my workplace too, and as Christians we must respect each other's space."

As a production worker, he couldn't handle the fact that I was an electrician and not subject to his orders. It frustrated him and was a blow to his ego. He'd had the opportunity to take the Skilled Trades test, just as I did. I sacrificed a lot for my trade. His jealousy of me caused a lot of unnecessary friction. I asked many managers to have him turn the volume down. They just laughed. From that point on, I tried to ignore him, just as I ignored so much of what was going on in this plant. Since I like some country music, I later brought some in and played it loud. Henry would come over to my station and give me glaring looks, but there was nothing he could do.

A woman on the MIG welder, Serena, was trained and responsible for visually checking welds and catching bad ones. Two robots operated in the cell, which is a fence-enclosed work area. The first placed the hinges and doors in position for welding, and the second removed the completed doors and placed them on the conveyor to move through the system. The supervisors came to me and ordered me to check the welds for Serena. I explained to them that I was an electrician and hadn't received any formal training to check welds, since that is a production job. The corporation had specially-trained weld monitors who used instruments to make certain the welds would hold in the event of a car accident. No consumer would be safe in a vehicle where welds were inspected by me. Serena came to me almost every half hour crying that the welder was producing bad welds. She was guessing. The management continually pressured me to assure her that her welds were good. I kept my MIG welder clean and well maintained to produce good welds and refused to baby-sit a grown woman. She had a production group leader for her needs.

It seemed to me that these GM managers were willing to put consumers at risk by trying to force me to tell this trained woman that the welds were good. By telling me to check the welds, GM seemed ready to commit negligence. If the welds were defective, this GM management would blame me for the defective welds. They hated me that much. I, on the other hand, placed the consumers at the top. On March 14, 2014 it was announced on the news that GM knew about defective ignition switches on a variety of cars in 2001. They did nothing, and consumers lost their lives because of the malfunctioning switches. After what I saw with the welds, it didn't surprise me. On March 31, 2014 GM announced a recall because of faulty power steering.

There was a major breakdown one day on my partner's welder, and I was assisting him. I needed to gain access to the 480-volts panel, but Serena's chair was blocking the entrance. Her chair prevented the door from being opened. When I asked her to move, she angrily replied, "I'm on my break and I'm not moving." Management ordered us to work around her, regardless of the danger. For safety reasons, her chair, or anything else, should not have blocked a 480-volt panel. Management should have ordered her to move the chair and never block the panels again, but they did not. They watched while my partner and I worked in danger. Her head was leaning on the 480 volt panel box. We could only slightly open the panel box. Management expected us to put our hands in a 480-volt high amperage fuse panel box to keep her from getting upset. If you reached in the panel box and touched the fuses, it would likely kill you. If she was leaning her head against the panel box and it exploded, she would have been lucky to have a head left.

The men would scream at Serena. I heard one electrician yell at her, "Leave me the fuck alone!" I saw her hug him later, trying to sweeten up his disposition. He in turn grabbed her, pulled her up on him, rubbed her up and down on his torso, and squeezed and caressed her buttocks, simulating a sexual encounter. When he released her, she was in as much shock as I was. She may have been annoying but that provocative display was disgusting. I watched as she walked around looking embarrassed for the remainder of the night.

When I returned to my main line, the big man, Henry, had been on a tirade. The only production woman who worked in the department told me that he had pushed her. She remained quiet because her husband worked in the body shop as well and she did not want a confrontation between them. Her husband was no match for him physically. Henry was huge and he used his size and deep, booming voice to intimidate people.

I began experiencing flare-ups with my MS. My legs would freeze and I couldn't walk. I climbed a ladder to access a job in the screen guard, an area above the machines with metal screen that it was safe to walk on. When I reached the top, my legs froze. I fought the panic, pulled myself around with the hand bars on the platform and willed myself to walk. I feared I would never walk again if I didn't move at that exact moment. I was alone in an isolated area where no one could see or hear me. It was up to me to get myself out of the situation, and I managed to do it.

In November, 1998, I began weekly injections of Avonex, an FDA approved drug to slow the progression of Multiple Sclerosis. The blindness in my eye had already left negative projections for my future. I normally experienced flu-like symptoms. I decided to take the injections at different times of the day to see when they would have the least impact on my work. One night I took the injection and reported to work.

My line ran spare parts until around 3:30 in the morning. My partner slept all night. When my line completed its job for the night, a maintenance supervisor from another line ordered me to change a transformer in his area. I still had to prepare my line for the first hour of the production shift. Most of the men were idle all night, while I worked steadily. Where was the man who was responsible for this line?

The supervisor, a large man, stood over me and barked, "I need you to change the transformer, without delay, right now." His size was intimidating, but I was more appalled by his actions. My partner was still snoring. I was excused from this job only because I had taken my MIG welder apart for maintenance, and the supervisor knew I had to reassemble it before production started up in the morning. I was becoming angry and tired of being the only one targeted to do others' work. We were all paid the same hourly rate. I received no compensation for doing more work than the men.

A few weeks later, after taking my injection, I began suffering from the flu-like side effects. Production was not running that night, so my going home shouldn't have been an issue. My supervisor asked me to stay and run my line. Other electricians should have been capable of running my line, including my partner whose line was not running. My line was the only line running spare parts that weekend. I agreed to stay despite feeling ill.

After we were done, around 4 a.m., the supervisor said, "I need you to change a motor on the MIG welder." My partner was still asleep. I told the supervisor, "I only stayed because you wanted me to run spare parts. Changing the motor will cause me to overheat. I'm ill and I need to go home." He then asked if I would stay and perform routine maintenance on my line, knowing I would do everything possible to keep my line running smoothly. I agreed to stay, changed cables and switches, and somehow finished out the night.

At the end of the night, supervisors must turn in a sheet showing if the job was done. After the supervisor turned in his maintenance report, the job order resurfaced. It had been turned in as "not completed." It had been completed, but the maintenance supervisor had failed to mark it so. Someone had written, "Motor too heavy for Camille" on the work order. The electricians who wouldn't do any work themselves started making negative comments about women in the trades. They had the pack mentality. I saw the sheet where Roland had written "BULLSHIT" next to the statement that the motor was too heavy for me. The motor was a fractional horsepower motor, something that electricians rig without help. It didn't weigh over 15 lbs. Electricians are responsible for carrying and mounting small motors. I was harassed for something I never said, by men who refused to work, themselves. The motor had already been changed. Again, management had no idea what was happening on the different lines of the body shop.

We were working 14-hour days. I worked all I could because I was scared to slow my pace. I wanted to keep my body moving. Everyone else worked 14 hours, but there was a difference: I actually worked them; the other guys were being punched out by their friends. Management took the path of least resistance. Every time they needed someone to run a line, I would get the first call.

Most of the guys had a friend in the "card club," which I never joined, to take care of their time. A card club consisted of a group of workers who agreed to punch each other in and out. There were time clocks all over the plant, and workers did not have to pass through a turnstile. Punching others' time clocks was extremely easy since the cards were swiped through a card scanner. This was my third GM plant and I'd never been exposed to this type of behavior before. Management knew these employees were defrauding the company, but instead of disciplining them, they made me the targeted employee. I refused to participate in the card club, and was warned that if I worked in the paint department, I would have to punch cards or face possible physical retribution.

I reported to work at 7:00 p.m., and worked until 9:30 the next morning. Chad Richards, who ran my area on second shift, started leaving this job to me earlier and earlier during his scheduled shift time. I was not there to allow Chad to use me. One day I entered the work area as soon as I arrived, and he was waiting for me.

"I need to go home. My wife called and I have to leave."

I just stared at him.

He put his tools away and said, "I'm gone."

"Hold it, Chad. No supervisor has given me instructions to relieve you to go home. This is your shift and your responsibility. You need to get a supervisor to tell me to take over your line."

His supervisor was standing there on the other side of the department. Chad had to ask the supervisor if he could leave, which meant he had to punch out. He was livid. He wanted me to work his shifts so could that he could get paid for not being there. He had only been with the company two years and I was a veteran with over 20 years at GM.

We all had areas of responsibilities to change welding caps and reset the steppers, which gradually increased the current during the welding process to compensate for wear on the electrodes. Weld caps are copper tips on the welding robots. They have to be changed after a certain number of welds. Each weld is considered a step. Each time a welding cap is changed, the count is reset to zero until the cap reaches the end of its life. When the caps can no longer produce good welds, the machine is at the end of the stepper. The welder for which Chad was responsible was pro-grammed to run approximately 12 hours. Working the third shift, I started working four hours after Chad should have changed tips on his welder. If he changed weld caps four hours into his eight hour shift, his welder should never have run out of weld counts a half hour into my shift.

Derek always visited me, and we both talked about how Chad failed to take care of his responsibility. When a tip change showed up on the marquee as a fault or a malfunction, Derek said, "I thought that station was Chad's responsibility." I replied, "It is. He doesn't change his station a lot."

Every electrician complained when he or she had to do the previous shift's work. Derek, who had been trying to get me to sleep with him, took it upon himself to confront Chad. He shouldn't have interfered. I didn't ask for his help. I could speak for myself. He had spoken for me, and then left me with the ramifications of his actions. He was doing this a lot, as I came to find out.

One evening, a few days later when I reported to work, Chad backed me into a corner and yelled, "I heard you're telling people I'm not doing my job." Being confronted by Derek had angered him. Chad was a wrestler and I knew I was out-matched without a weapon. I backed away from him to avoid an altercation. My physical health was deteriorating and I was not mentally ready to deal with this irate man. I had just learned from my neurologist that I might have Raynaud's Disease, a circulatory problem in which blood vessels become constricted, decreasing blood supply to the fingers causing them to turn pale or blue, and painful.

When I saw Derek, I told him he was making life harder for me. I pleaded with him to cease and desist. He was not my husband and he had no right speaking for me. He was always trying to impress me. He bragged about being ambidextrous, although I never saw evidence of it. He gave me a CD he had made, and said he played all the instruments on it. The music was mediocre, at best. I didn't even like this type of music, preferring classical music. I gave the CD back. Derek thought he was being my hero by giving his opinion on the way I was being treated by others; but when they became angry about it, they took it out on me. It was a body shop rumor that Derek was trying to sleep with me, so working with him was a sickening and frustrating experience.

A few days later, Derek was asleep and I was sitting upstairs in the Cab area, where we both worked. He was drunk and the alcohol had caused him to go to sleep. I was quiet when I first entered the area, but when I smelled the alcohol I bumped a chair and woke him up. He rolled over and looked at me with lustful eyes.

"I love sex," he said while licking his lips at me.

I ignored him.

"I love sex," he repeated, still looking lustfully at me.

"Yeah, that's nice," I replied, wishing he would go back to sleep.

"I love all kinds of sex. Last night I was muff-diving (his term for oral sex)." He told me that he met this woman on the Internet. Yuck.

"That's nice, but you get nothing here. I have a husband and I'm not interested in you. You sleep with anyone, and that's disgusting to me. Leave me alone." I left the area. I didn't need to hear him describing his sexual experiences. He would often get high or drunk and want to describe his sexual escapades to me. The drugs and alcohol loosened his inhibitions. He had no shame. Some of the things he said to me were disturbing and disgusting. He was just as bad as that nasty man, Sam, the drunken electrician at American Axle, who told me I would have to "eat his shit." Sam also wanted me to hear about sexual things he did with women.

When I first met Derek, I was speaking with a group of electricians. Derek sauntered over to introduce himself. He stood about 5'4", weighed around 130 lbs, and had teeth that needed a good cleaning. I stand 5'6" and weigh 130 lbs. He had a few brains, but he was more interested in using his small brain on the women he worked with. He had just been divorced a short time and was now going wild sleeping with women. I wanted no more than a working relationship with him. He wanted more.

The management loved Derek because he would do anything they wanted. If no one else would do it, he would. He seemed to have a need for approval. Essentially, he was a "yes man" with little self-respect. In turn, management ignored his daily, dangerous substance abuse on the job. At times I saw him so high it was a wonder how he made it past the guards. He would stumble into the department and fall into a drug and alcohol-induced stupor.

Derek told me a little about himself as I grew to know him. He had three kids, and said he had gotten his ex-wife hooked on drugs. He was living and sleeping with her best friend, and his children were living with his mother. I told him I had been married for 15 years, had a little girl, and had been with my husband for twenty years.

By the time I met Derek his morals were already sorely compromised, and they got worse. Derek came across as a narcissist whose life was driven by sex, drugs, and alcohol. He bragged to me that he had already slept with five women in the plant. The drugs and alcohol gave him the courage to tell me about his sexual habits. He seemed to view any Black woman he wanted to have sex with as his personal sex toy to do with as he pleased. He didn't care if the woman was married or in a long-term relationship. He wanted what he wanted and would take extreme measures to get it, including violence, which he would demonstrate later. He had no regard for the women he hurt.

Since Derek was teased so often about his height, it seemed that his way of proving his manhood was by sleeping with all the Black women he could. His eyes barely met mine as he ogled my body. One of the other electricians started snickering. I knew I was going to have a problem with Derek chasing me, and I was right. I saw him as an extremely weak, insecure man who needed approval from his friends, and figured if I explained that I was married and not interested, that would be sufficient. I was woefully wrong. The knowledge that I was married just made me seem more of a challenge. I think from the moment we met, Derek thought of nothing else but gazing into my green eyes, caressing my body, having passionate sex with me, and listening to me telling him what a wonderful lover he was. I think I was the first green-eyed Black woman that he had ever met, and he was not going to pass up an opportunity to sleep with one. The thought consumed him, but it made me want to upchuck. He tried everything to get me to have sex with him, going from extreme niceness to extreme abusiveness. Even as his actions became violent and abusive, the UAW and GM protected him.

As we continued to work, there were new apprentices entering the trades. Most of them were relatives of the union leaders or management, and they came in with a sense of entitlement. If you want an apprentice to learn a trade, you place him or her with a qualified tradesman. Apprentices usually are assigned to the best people. Apparently, this management thought I was qualified to train an apprentice because I received an apprentice to train. My partner, Frank, was building his own house. He would work on it all day, and sleep at GM all night. He tried to make my apprentice do all of his work while he slept, and then he got upset with me because I would not allow it. Apprentices were there to gain knowledge so they could become an asset to the corporation, not for personal use. Unfortunately for some of the female apprentices, those who started sleeping with some of the men in the trades hoping for easier lives, it only worked until the men tired of them.

Eventually, I was bumped back to the first shift on the same line. Again I had supervisor Carlo to deal with. We were working 10-hour shifts during the week. Carlo told me he wanted me to stay on the line after my eight hours and help the afternoon shift guys.

I asked, "Are you making all the male electricians help afternoons, or just me?"

He hesitated, but did not force the third shift electrician to help me, although he was working 10 hours as well.

"You stay in this area and help Chad and Alan, and respond to their calls."

"Fine, but where are the other electricians working over in this area? Everyone working 10 hours should receive the same treatment."

There were two electricians assigned to these lines on their shift: Chad and his drugged, alcoholic partner, Alan. It was their responsibility to run their line. If Carlo O'Toole forced me to stay, he wouldn't have to force the men to do their work or deal with their volatile behavior. This did not seem fair to me, and I approached the maintenance superintendent, Jack Tolbin, to tell him what was happening and that Carlo O'Toole was putting unnecessary pressure on me. It was the only conversation concerning my Multiple Sclerosis I ever had with him.

He looked astonished, "You have MS?"

"Yes, didn't my union steward, Bill Coffey, speak with you about it?"

"No, he didn't. I had no idea you have MS. You don't exhibit it."

"I try to do the best I can with the disease, but I don't need the excess stress. Please speak to Carlo O'Toole about his unfairness."

My union steward, Bill Coffey, had never spoken with Jack although he told me he had. Right after that conversation, in the fall of 1999, I was bumped to the second shift. Derek had once again approached me while high on drugs, and said, "Ha-ha-ha. Alan is going to bump your ass."

"What? I asked.

"I talked to him and he's going to bump your ass to afternoons. Ha-ha-ha."

Derek was doing everything he could to make my life miserable. He knew I wanted to stay on days. But Alan shouldn't have listened to Derek. He did bump me, but later lost his job on the first shift. More managers work the first shift, so there were more eyes to witness what he was doing. From this point on, though, my life took a desperate turn, and the man who tried to use me, Chad, played a big role in it.

What a joke

Workplace Violence Prevention

People are most productive at work when all distractions have been minimized. Leaders commit to providing an organizational direction and the proper tools for people to focus on their work responsibilities and maximize their productivity. Another important factor is feeling safe and secure in the work environment.

General Motors is committed to protecting the health and safety of each resident by providing a work environment that is free from harassment, threats and acts of violence.

Workplace Violence is defined as: "Any act occurring in the workplace or arising out of the work-related activities which results in threatened or actual harm to persons or property".

In support of this initiative and consistent with our health and safety policy, GM will not tolerate any threat, direct or implied, or physical conduct by any person which results in harm to people or property, or which disrupts, or interferes with another's work performance, or which creates an intimidating, offensive or hostile environment.

Some examples of workplace violence are:

- The threat or physical assault against another
- Stalking or continuous harassment of another person causing terror, fear, worry or intimidation
- Actions aimed at disrupting business operations
- Indirect threats
- Direct threats

Employees can contribute to maintaining a safe work environment by following these guidelines:

- Maintain control of your own emotions and refrain from making threatening statements, even those made as a joke
- Be supportive of your co-workers
- Be willing to cooperate in resolving concerns in situations or relationships
- Utilize employee support programs
- Bring to your supervisor's attention any person identified as being a risk

Each facility should develop a local procedure in the event that a workplace violence incident happens at their location. This plan should include the following:

- Establishing a process for evaluating threats and/or violent behavior
- Defining how a threat will be responded to
- Establishing local reporting Mechanisms (Supervisor, local management, local security and the GM Awareline)
- Ensuring a Post-Incident Response
- Communicating the local plan to all employees

Anyone who experiences an incident in which they feel someone is threatening them with harm should first take steps necessary to protect their safety and the safety of those around them. The only appropriate immediate action when confronting a violent person is to do what is necessary to protect oneself and then follow-up with the "local facility" procedures defined above.

CHAPTER 6

I reported to the same area on the afternoon shift that I'd worked on day shift, the door area. This time I worked for a production supervisor by the name of Adrian. He was an ex-production group leader who had always tried to order me around when he worked in that capacity. As a production group leader, he was in charge of production workers only. Production workers were unskilled workers who assembled the cars. No previous experience was required for their job. As soon as he made supervisor, Adrian made a beeline for me. He tried to impress me that he was now a supervisor, but I knew he was still unqualified to supervise my work. His degree was in Social Work. He had no training in maintenance, especially electrical or any other trade. One day I was checking out a robot fault and had to leave the power on to see the signals.

I had almost traced the fault down when he came running over in a panic yelling, "The MIG welder is down."

"Adrian, I'm on a job that needs to come up immediately."

"Get to the MIG now!" he shouted.

I dropped what I was doing and did as he ordered. He was absolutely right; the MIG welder was no longer running. The area was full of completed doors, and no more doors were able to pass through. I had a "full bank," as we refer to it. As supervisor, Adrian should have been able to look up at the conveyor and make the determination, himself, that the bank was full and that no more doors could pass through. He was angry and yelling at me because the MIG welder was not running, and it couldn't run because the bank was full. When I returned to my original job, he followed, still shouting at me because he felt free to abuse me. He only abused the women; he feared other men. As a result, I walked into precisely what I had been searching for, an electrified wire that had come loose. Among a tangle of hanging wires, the exposed wire wasn't visible. Distracted by Adrian's shouting, I hadn't seen it, and it electrocuted me.

Adrian entered a cell I was working in a few days later and made life hazardous for me again by tossing around scrapped parts that needed to be removed. He was upset because none of the production group leaders had removed them. When he had been a production group leader it had been his job to remove the scrap parts. Now the current group leader was not doing his job, and it made Adrian angry. The edges of the metal could slice your skin open if you bumped into it, and here he was throwing sharp material around. I didn't want the scrap metal to cut me or the wires on the equipment, so I asked for a union steward to write a safety grievance. Adrian got upset and ordered me to move the scrap, which was mostly truck doors weighing 52 lbs each, more than 2/5 of my body weight. I tried to move them but they were too heavy. I asked Adrian to call the UAW safety rep. He became nervous and, I believe, not wanting a safety grievance written against him, he never placed my call.

Safety grievances are usually taken very seriously. MiOSHA (Michigan Occupational Safety and Health Administration) investigates workplace accidents and has the power to shut down unsafe operations. All requests for union officials must go through the management. When I spoke later with the safety rep, he didn't explain why he hadn't come when I asked

Adrian to call him. He informed me I had a 35-pound weight restriction without a hoist. I later learned that the weight limit was actually 25 pounds for a woman.

The supervisor who had thrown the condom into my area approached me a few days later. "Camille, we are getting poor tip dressing on the pedestal welder. I need you to correct this situation."

"I can only change welding caps to produce good welds."

"Correct this problem at once! You are responsible for the robot," he said.

He was right; it was my responsibility to change caps and reset the steppers. The robot cords were my responsibility for electrical maintenance purposes and for changing tips. But the problem was not an electrical problem. Besides that, it concerned a fixture pedestal welder, which had to be repaired by a machine repairman. I didn't have the knowledge, tools, or skills to repair it. It took quite a while for it to sink in that there was nothing I could do. He had to call the properly-trained trade. He was so busy ordering me around, he wasn't listening to what I was telling him.

A few days later, we had a problem on a weld gun. From my perspective, I could see a bolt on the gun knocking into my electrical shunt. When the machine repairmen arrived, I tried to explain to them and to my supervisor what the problem was, but everyone ignored me. The company absorbed the cost of the down time while the machine repairmen took the gun off for repair. Two days later, they returned the gun and installed it. The same problem surfaced. Taking a closer look, they determined that the bolt on the gun was hitting the shunt. I was used to excessive downtime because management did not respect the fact that I was a qualified electrician and knew what I was talking about. This downtime was unnecessary.

The supervisor even said he should have listened to me. The problem was visible, I had pointed it out, and they had chosen to ignore me once again.

In the fall of 1999, I was working in an area with men who were having problems with their wives and girlfriends. Coupled with the fact that my partner was now Chad, and that he was not pleased with me either, it didn't make a very pleasant atmosphere for me

Chad was stealing from the company. One day, he stole a new large roll of S/O cord. S/O cord is a cable that has a number of wires enclosed in a rubber jacket, and is used for temporary electrical power connections. You choose the right size S/O cord for the job at hand. Chad walked the roll of cord right out the back gate with the security guards present. When he returned to the area, he had strained his back and was visibly in pain. He wanted to file a Worker's Compensation claim against the company. He grimaced and said, "I hurt my back putting that cord in my truck. I think I'm going to file for Worker's Comp."

"Hmm," I said.

"I need you to vouch for me."

"Huh?"

"I need you to witness I hurt my back working in the cell."

"I can't do that."

"What do you mean, you can't do it? We're partners!"

"I can't lie for you."

He looked at me, cursed under his breath, and fumed as he slunk away. I was not going to help him defraud the company and steal from them. He could find one of his friends to do it for him. Even if I would consider such corrupt behavior, I knew that if it ever became an issue, I would get fired and he would be protected at all cost. We were "partners" as long as I was willing to allow him to use me, and I refused to comply.

There was one bright spot, though. An electrician by the name of Joshua Noble maintained one of the lines. He was a fair man and everyone liked him. He didn't curse and didn't like what he witnessed happening to me. He knew I came to work every day and did my job. Like me, he was a transplant. The transplanted electricians had previous exposure to minorities and women, and thought differently. We clicked as friends. I considered him my work angel. I was fortunate that I was not completely alone while surrounded by so much hostility.

Chad and my future tormenter, Stan, were friends. They worked the same line now, Chad on afternoons and Stan on midnights. Stan came in early and Chad left early. It was an agreement between friends and I preferred to stay out of it. My first memory of Stan was of him sprawled out drunk in the electrician's crib. Supervisors and other electricians just ignored him. Like Derek, he was a short guy who used women to boost his ego. Although he was married, he was carrying on a torrid affair with a married woman whose husband also worked at the plant. Derek, Stan and Chad all were short men. Not one was over 5'4". It bothered them that I stood over them. They wouldn't take on other men, but they could take on a small woman with MS. The taller men really picked on the shorter men, and here I was, taller than they were. There was one guy who stood around 4'11". He was teased unmercifully. When I came along, he said to me, "You remind me of my little wife with her little toolbox." I looked at him and laughed to myself. My toolbox was the same size as his and I was 7 inches taller than he.

Chad asked me, "Did you see the woman put a note in Stan's toolbox?" As I turned, a curly haired, blond woman was staring at me. She was Stan's married lover. Chad was laughing so hard, she left. All of his friends in the body shop knew and often talked about it. Some even knew the line her husband worked on.

Chad said, "Take it out, read it, and tell me what it says." I refused. When I returned to the area to clean my welder, the note was on the floor. I picked it up and stuck it back in Stan's toolbox. When he arrived at work, I let him know that his note had fallen on the floor and he needed to retrieve it before someone else did. He grabbed me, extremely happy, and hugged me hard, hurting me.

I screamed, "Let go of me, now!"

He reeked of alcohol and I knew he was intoxicated. His eyes were so big, I suspected he had also taken cocaine. He released his hold on me and stared at me in disbelief. He was not accustomed to women rejecting him. I hurried away.

Chad came back to me and asked, "Did you read the note?"

"No."

Chad had wanted me to read the note. He then would tell Stan I had read it.

A few days later, I went to retrieve some tools from my toolbox. When I entered our little area, Stan and this lady were hugged up and seemed oblivious to the fact this was a work area. I quietly backed out of the area and let them continue. I decided to retrieve my tools and do the job I needed them for later. There was a cabinet where I kept my everyday working tools, and I didn't need to go to my toolbox often. It had been sitting in the same place for almost a year, not bothering anyone.

A week later, Chad approached me and said, "Have you talked to Stan?"

I answered, "No."

Chad said, "He wants your toolbox moved. He wants that space."

"Chad, my box has been in the same place for almost a year. Stan had plenty of time to claim that space as his own before I arrived in the area. Obviously, he had no need for it before this time, since my box had been here so long. There is not enough room on the other side. We must share what little space we have. Do *not* touch my toolbox."

Some of the men had four or five toolboxes. I had one file cabinet that I used as a toolbox. It was a daily battle for me it to protect my tradesman tools and the space allotted to me. Thanksgiving holiday came, and I was off for the weekend. When I returned to work, my toolbox was missing. I searched for it and found it shoved into the area where the electrician on the midnight shift had kept his toolbox. His toolbox was gone.

Dirk, another electrician, came to visit me and helped to move my toolbox to its original spot. As we were conversing after finishing the move, Chad entered the department. He was being punched in at 11a.m. and getting to the job shortly before 3 p.m. When he saw my toolbox in its original position, he rushed into my area wanting to confront me. Seeing Dirk, he stopped dead in his tracks, his mouth dropped, and he backed up and left.

Dirk looked at me puzzled and asked, "What was that?"

I said, "He is waiting for you to leave before he confronts me. He wants me by myself."

I was right. As soon as Dirk rounded the corner out of sight, Chad pounced on me. He started yelling, "We were doing you a favor by moving your toolbox."

"What you did was sneaky and underhanded, and you know better to touch another tradesman's toolbox. You moved my toolbox into Frank's spot," I said.

Because I had previously backed off when these guys were nasty to me, I guess Chad thought I would run away again; but I held my ground. He walked off, enraged, giving me the OK sign with his fingers. I knew he was waiting to send Stan my way when he reported to work.

I was sitting in my area talking to my supervisor, Danny, when Stan arrived. Danny had been getting complaints that Chad was not responding fast enough to the faults on his line. His solution was to have us take turns on either line.

I said, "This is not fair to me. I am taking care of my line. Instead of penalizing me, you should be talking to Chad about his response time. Are you going to discipline me because Chad refuses to do his job?"

Instead of addressing the situation, Danny decided to take the easy way out and shift the burden to me. He knew I would not allow the line to be down long. As we spoke, Stan charged into my area, yelling at me, with clenched fists. He glanced over at the supervisor, but that did not deter him. I was in shock, and feared he would strike me. He was screaming, inebriated, and more than likely under the influence of cocaine. I also smelled marijuana. I sought assistance from my supervisor, who was sitting there observing this. He looked at Stan, then me, and then this General Motors supervisor rose out of his chair, and ran. I was stunned. He left me alone to deal with this drunken, drugged-out, volatile man.

Seeing this, Stan really vented his rage, screaming, "Why do you have to be such a hard ass?"

He was inches from my face, growing red with rage. In fear, I tried calmly talking to him, all the while searching for a way around him. I had a hammer and an awl in my possession at all times. Had he attacked me I would have defended my life. My other self-defense option would have been to grab the screwdriver at my workbench and plunge it into his neck.

I gripped my hammer. I was not going to let him hurt me or keep me as his hostage, but he was blocking my exit. I had no way out of the area. He was upon me before I knew it. Screaming in my face, he threatened to place my toolbox on the next train out of the plant.

Suddenly, the alarms began to sound. My robot had crashed. As I tried to maneuver around Stan while gripping the handle of my hammer hidden in my apron, he pointed his finger inches from my face and yelled, "You are out of here!"

At this point, our voices had attracted the attention of a few of the production men, and now they were watching him. One stopped dead in his tracks to see if I needed help. Stan saw him and became afraid. It was obvious he did not want to deal with the men. He exited my area, walked the 17 feet to his area, and shoved my toolbox into the aisle. He was in a complete rage. I was stunned. This was the first time I faced a physical threat at work.

After I recovered from the initial shock, I proceeded to take care of my robot. As I was working, Heath, the general foreman, came to my area, and I explained what happened. His only recourse was to force Stan to move my box back. The drugs and alcohol were ignored. This just added to Stan's fury. When I returned to my area, he paraded around with rage clearly visible on his face. He gave me hateful and intimidating looks and made gestures with his hands indicating he wanted to chop my head off.

Chad, in the meantime, was having a great laugh at my expense. He was a master manipulator. He didn't want any trouble himself, so he pushed Stan into it. Stan was like putty in his hands. I passed by Stan several times during the night. Each time, he glared at me viciously and drew his finger across his throat. From that day on, he greeted me with the same attitude and the same glares of hateful intimidation. He began to stalk me, and I began to believe he would assault me. He was always under the influence of drugs and alcohol, which clouded his thinking.

A week later, I went to retrieve tools for a special job from my toolbox before Stan came in. I was with my friend Joshua. I tried to open my lock but had trouble with the key. As I checked to make sure I had the right key, Joshua looked at my locks. Someone had taken Loc-tite glue, which is always available in the plant, and glued my locks. We found a small bottle of Loc-tite in Stan's area. I called the maintenance supervisor and he called the millwrights to bring bolt cutters. My personal property was destroyed. The supervisor gave me GM safety locks, which are for the equipment only and are never to be used on toolboxes. Employees face discipline if they use them on anything else but lock-out. Violated again, I now had to be concerned about which supervisor was going to discipline me for "improper use of safety locks."

At this point, I had begun to fear for my safety. There were rumors floating around that I was due for a dousing of 5-10 gallons of water from the ceiling. This was a popular prank among the guys. With my small frame, I knew I'd be knocked to the floor. Grown men crashed to the floor when water was poured on them from above. I worried what the impact would have on my Multiple Sclerosis. I began to carry salt in tissues that I kept in my apron at all times. I had decided to fling some in Stan's eyes to make my escape if he attacked me. I wanted to avoid striking him in the head with the hammer, but I would defend my life. I also carried a screwdriver and awl at all times. If Stan assaulted me, I would plunge one of them into his neck. It was bad to think like that, but I was not going to allow him to hurt me. It was that serious.

The midnight superintendent for production, Gary Sprew, set up an appointment with GM Labor Relations to discuss my concerns. He seemed nervous about this, but he was the only one who tried to assist me. I fought with myself over ratting on two union brothers, but the rationale was that they ceased to be my union brothers when they began to harass me. This is where I met Labor Relations Rep. Victor Longella. I told him about the terror I felt.

He asked, "Are you the one Gary sent?"

"Yes," I replied.

"Umm, you're not at all what I expected," he said, slowly looking me over.

He obviously was not expecting an intelligent, well-spoken Black woman. I shook off the negative feelings that were enveloping me and concentrated on the task ahead. I told him I wanted the harassment stopped. I explained that I had MS and that the added stress and fear could cause an exacerbation of my illness from which I might not recover. While I was speaking with Mr. Longella, I smelled alcohol on his breath.

When the interview was completed he escorted me to the door and said, "Thanks for coming in. I'll handle it."

After the interview, the intimidation escalated. Stan began reporting to work at 7 p.m. As soon as he arrived he made a beeline for me. He would walk past my area as much as he could, purposely run into me in the aisle, and stare at me with tightly clenched teeth and fists. When he was sure no one was looking, he would draw his finger across his throat and point at me.

I had met a few friendly coworkers. My friend, Peter Westly, was there with me one day. Peter was maintaining the opposite line. When Stan came in, he immediately began harassing me. Peter silently watched him. When Stan finally saw Peter, he backed off. Many abusive men retreat as soon as another man is present. I think I was the only electrician Stan could beat in a fight.

I asked an ex-manager how long it should take before Labor responded to my complaint. He said they should have returned to me immediately. It never happened, though. I never spoke with Victor Longella again. I knew I was in big trouble.

Every day when Stan arrived, I called for the supervisors to come around and check on my safety. They all knew what was going on, but for some reason they refused to stop it. No one interceded on my behalf. Once again, I placed a call to my union steward, even though the union hated union-against-union cases. I needed intervention from my union. When the union steward appeared, I asked him to send the Civil Rights representative to see me. He never showed up. The Civil Rights rep was supposed to look out for minorities and women who felt they were being abused on the job. I knew I was completely on my own. During this time, the only way the union Civil Rights rep could see you was if the union steward deemed it necessary. In the anti-minority atmosphere I was dealing with in this plant, I knew I didn't stand a chance. From this point on, the harassment intensified.

I told the general foreman that he could send me to the worst line we had, but I wanted to be removed from this hostile environment. Instead of moving me, management decided to move Chad. The Black general foreman moved a Black male into Chad's spot. I could not understand his reasoning and asked him about it. It was not this man's job to protect me from Stan, it was GM's.

He said, "If Stan sees David working here, he will be hesitant to attack you." That was no solution! David would have stopped Stan had he attacked me, but he should never have been placed in a position to jeopardize his own job. I asked the Black general foreman, Amos, why no one in management was interceding on my behalf. He said, "Bill Pettiman told me to leave it alone." Bill was also a superintendent. Amos became visibly nervous after telling me this.

All they had to do was move me, but they refused. And now Stan was angry that management had moved his friend.

An Infrared job came open and a general foreman offered it to me based on my high seniority. Infrared involves using a heat-detecting camera that shows the hot spots in the equipment. Since early detection helps to prevent major break-downs, with infrared I would be able to find malfunctions in the equipment by locating areas of overheating. I accepted the job. I figured it was a good job, and it would move me away from Chad and Stan. Since we were all doing 14 hours, I reported to work at 11 a.m., and trained with the first shift electrician, Prince, who was already a level II thermographer.

On January 18, 2000, I reported to work. Before I ventured into my area, my friend Joshua stopped me. He wanted to warn me before I saw the latest development in the campaign of harassment against me. Apparently, there was a picture posted in the department of a dead rodent in the street, with the caption "ROADKILL" underneath. Someone had written my name on it. I became more frightened and took it as a threat on my life. Now I was scared to go to my car at night. I still could not get management to help.

Training for the Infrared job would take place in Boston, Massachusetts, the week of February 14, 2000. I had submitted all the paperwork, and everything was approved. The week before I was to depart, one of the supervisors, Percy Skeeter, told me he had bad news for me.

He said, "Your class has been canceled due to inclement weather."

"How do you know what the weather will be like a week from now?"

"Sorry, your class is cancelled," he said as he walked off with a smirk on his face.

A third shift electrician who had just returned from a union-appointed position was taking my Infrared job. This union rep was an electrician and a union appointee. He was also a supporter of Donny Douglas, the union official convicted of extorting from GM. He had been on a special job given to him by the union. In the meantime, the union had eliminated the job he had been doing previously. When he lost his union job, he demanded my Infrared job. GM management refused to answer my questions about why I was being replaced, and returned me to the line without further explanation. I felt I was being set up for the harassment to continue. How could anyone know what the weather was going to be that week, which was weeks away? I was returned to the hostile environment I had sought to escape. Stan continued to terrorize me, against GM's stated policy. I was becoming more and more frustrated.

One night, an area Superintendent and the general foreman caught Stan and four of his friends drinking on the job. Management only disciplined one of them. They were all alcoholics, but management liked Alan the least, so he was the one they disciplined. Alan was also the one Derek convinced to bump me. Alan had to pee in a cup on demand to keep his job, since his drug addiction was that bad. He couldn't stay out of trouble on first shift, and eventually lost his job. Stan was not disciplined, and I wondered if it was because his father-in-law owned an electrical business that sometimes did work for GM. Stan continued to stalk me and place himself in my field of vision while making threatening gestures whenever he could. I had no one to turn to.

CHAPTER 7

In August of 2000, there was a news report about a KKK incident in a GM plant. I said to my husband, "It's probably my plant." Sure enough, as I watched the news a picture of the plant appeared. I was stunned but not surprised. It seems a group leader had crudely fashioned a KKK outfit out of a work uniform, and had approached a couple of Black men. He told them that he was the Grand Wizard of the KKK, and said, "You niggers need to get your shit together." When they reported the incident to Labor Relations, it was investigated by Victor Longella. GM Labor Relations said that nothing happened. It was only when the Black employees went to the NAACP of North Oakland County that another investigation was launched and GM admitted that this incident had, indeed, occurred.

Mr. H. Wallace Parker, legal counsel for the Oakland branch of the NAACP, initially sought justice for the employees. I started hearing rumors that the NAACP wanted to interview other minority employees who were experiencing problems at this plant. I was one of them. Stan did not stop his harassment, but he toned it down a bit. I waited for the NAACP to contact me, but they never did. Our attorney later told us that GM had told the NAACP to stand down because GM gives them a million dollars a year.

During the summer, the Queen, the White, female electrician approached me. We were both transplanted electricians. The male electricians nicknamed her the Queen because she did not have to follow the rules. She was treated like royalty by GM management, and did as she pleased. She complained that her son had failed his math class and she needed to work the afternoon shift, which would enable her to drive him to summer school during the day. I wanted to trade shifts with her; but, again, management had other ideas. They decided that since I was not in Control Support, I could not trade with her. Control Support electricians were specially trained to be the troubleshooters in the Body Shop. If an electrician couldn't figure out a problem, they called Control Support.

Instead, they selected Todd, a man with two years at GM, and allowed him to work the first shift. Todd's father worked at the UAW headquarters in a high ranking job with the international union. Todd and I had worked together at American Axle, and had gotten along wonderfully. After he was hired in Pontiac, and teamed up with Chad and Stan, I hardly knew him anymore. I complained. Shifts were served by seniority, in compliance with our contract.

Control Support is a coveted electrician's job, and I wanted to receive the special training necessary for this job. The Queen worked with the ABB experts for almost a year to become a specialist. ABB provided robots to GM, as well as the technical training in their use. Any electrician afforded the same opportunity could have learned just as well. I was happy for the Queen when she first started, but I learned she had ulterior motives. I was the only Black female journeyman electrician. The Queen was the only White female journeyman electrician in the Body Shop. The management favored her, and she used the power and influence she had over them. She would tell them lies about things I said, and they believed her. I hardly ever spoke with her. Management was clearly under her spell, and she ate it up.

After I complained, she angrily approached me and said, "I don't appreciate you complaining. I need to get my son to summer school."

"My seniority rights have been violated. When I wanted to attend school to better myself and benefit the company, I was denied the shift change. Your son fails his regular class and you are granted special privileges. Why?"

She angrily replied, "Things that happen to you, do not happen to me. I get what I want. I just wanted to let you know I don't appreciate you complaining."

The smile on her face as she left told me all I needed to know. My life became more difficult after our conversation. She fed management information on other employees, and things were attributed to me that I never said. This sick management thrived on idle gossip.

I then waited for the apprentices to graduate so I could bump one of them or a new hire. It was my daughter's first year of high school and I wanted to become more available to her. Most of the apprentices either knew someone or had a parent with connections. Most were extremely lazy. They learned just enough to be dangerous. One married female apprentice, who was having an affair with a married boss, would force bits on in the logic to complete a cycle. It was a dangerous thing to do. Bits are on and off switches. A cycle is a completed movement, like crossing the finish line. The logic is what makes the machines move. You must know the outcome of a move when you manipulate a bit. The robot had not been welding properly and she forced the bit on. Then she acted silly by grinning in the boss's face. I walked away shaking my head at the lack of safety all around.

Trying to bump one of the apprentices became extremely difficult. I submitted the required paper work and was told I had not submitted it in time. The next time I received this excuse, I produced a Xeroxed copy of my request to no avail. Then I learned that the apprentices were having an in-plant class. Management used this excuse not to honor seniority rights. Apparently, they did not know what an in-plant journeyman meant, nor did they care.

This management violated our National contract all the time without being challenged by the UAW. Although this was my third GM plant, we all abided by the same national agreement that was signed with the Corporate Management. We also had a local agreement to which the corporation agreed to adhere. This management blatantly disregarded and disrespected our negotiated contracts with the union and consistently bargained in bad faith. Finally, in the fall, I was able to bump a graduated apprentice and made it to the third shift.

In September 2000, general foreman, Dylan Lukumski, asked if I wanted to work Control Support. We agreed I would work with Derek, who was also in Control Support for training. Derek was an expert with the robots, but I came from a plant that didn't have robots. I was sitting in an area downstairs when the line went down. The station was at the end of its stepper and could weld no more. The welding caps had to be changed. The electrician on that line had been sent to school by management, and the managers were unaware they had no line coverage. I decided to be a good worker and change the caps. I did nothing but buy myself trouble.

I locked out the Monitored Power System (MPS) for the cell I was entering. After I turned the water off for the station, I climbed in. Looking up, I saw that the robot in the next cell was holding a part, and that I was standing in its drop-off path. If the robot moved, it would land on my head.

There was only a light-screen curtain to protect me. Light-screen curtains are not considered lock-out by MiOSHA and cannot be counted on for protection. The purpose of a light-screen curtain is to stop machines or workers from moving into another cell when they shouldn't, causing damage to equipment or injury and possible death to employees. Since they are controlled electrically, they can fail, so the area demanded a full power down. I have seen the curtains fail and the robots crash into things.

As I was changing tips, the production group leader showed up. He looked in, saw me, and ran to get his supervisor, Adrian. Production group leaders are untrained and unqualified to supervise me. Adrian ran over and started yelling that I had shut down his line. I was inside the cell changing welding caps, and he was in an emotional frenzy. The marquee was flashing, "Station at end of stepper." Nothing else could be welded until the caps were changed. It was two hours into the shift, and management did not realize they were missing an electrician. I had been taking care of the line without direction. If I left the department, no one would know. I chose not to. I finished the job at hand, and exited the cell.

As I proceeded to get the line back up, Adrian was still yelling about me locking out the other cell. My supervisor, who should have intervened, was standing nearby and not saying a word.

Finally, I asked, "Adrian, what do you want me to do?"

He shouted, "I want my line back up."

"That's what I'm trying to do but you kept interfering and preventing me from getting the line up in a timely fashion."

"I don't like the way you locked out."

"Can't you see my head's in the robot's path? I don't want the robot landing on my head."

He ran to report me to another general foreman when I asked for a union rep. There were several managers in the group, but no one came near me because they knew I was right. Adrian was livid.

I had been working with Derek for approximately six weeks when the Queen approached. She seemed ready to instigate trouble, approaching me with a wicked smile on her face and asking if I knew what Derek had done. Apparently, Derek had e-mailed a couple of managers criticizing the way they were utilizing me. He did not like it when they had me running the lines and not training with him. I did not want him speaking for me.

With a smirk on her face the Queen said, "Management says you and Derek are too close." Management only knew how Derek felt about me. They didn't know that I felt nothing about Derek, and that he was merely a co-worker.

Her words angered me, and I replied, "You can have all the managers catering to your every whim, verbally ridicule them, direct nasty, abusive language their way, and that's OK; but I can't work with a Black man unless I'm sleeping with him. I love these double standards."

She walked away with a smile on her face. The Queen would call the managers "stupid assholes" and other nasty names over the in-plant radio. Another of her favorites was "dumb motherfuckers." None of them escaped her wrath. I looked for Derek and demanded that he stop emailing the managers.

"You are making my life hard," I yelled. "You have no right to say anything to management about my work. I can speak for myself and you had no right telling these managers what to do with me. Stop it!"

Derek did not understand boundaries. I didn't want people thinking I was sleeping with Derek. He wouldn't mind, but I did. I was six years older than Derek, more mature, definitely more educated and not interested in him in any way other than ordinary work relationship. Derek and I had no outside of work relationship. Instead of listening to him, Management should have told Derek to mind his own business.

When Derek and I met, I came with my own brains, my own finances, and a good husband. Derek looked at the two female supervisors and me as if we were his personal smorgasbord. He wanted to sample every item on the buffet. He had already tried two items, and he wanted the third. When he tried to exert control over me, I immediately put a stop to it. I repeatedly told him that he had no rights over me and that I would never sleep with him. It went in one ear and out the other. The other two knew he was trying his best to sleep with me. That created a little jealousy amongst them, and they began to treat me harshly. They had power over me. Derek told me that he liked uneducated "ghetto women" because they slept with him quicker. That was not me.

A few days after the Queen's visit, Derek and I had a conversation.

"Camille, I bought a Bible and I want to discuss it with you."

I stared at him and shook my head. "I am not discussing the Bible with you. You never go to church or read the Bible. Why would I discuss it with you?"

"I want to go over a few things with you," he said.

"I am not discussing the Bible with you. I hope you saved your receipt. You need to go get your money back."

I felt he was going to use the Bible to try to break down my inhibitions about sleeping with him. He was truly a sexual deviant who only cared about what he wanted in this world, and he badly wanted to sleep with me. What happened to me meant nothing to him as long as he got what he wanted; and he went go to extreme means to get what he wanted. I believe he was a narcissist.

I was told to change caps on a station that the regular electricians did not change according to the tip-changing schedule. I wasn't able to reach the caps, so I moved to a better vantage point. Suddenly, a heavy piece of steel equipment called a "dump" drifted in and slammed into the spot where I would have been standing in. I could have sustained a head injury or a broken neck. No doubt, I would have been badly injured, or even killed. The experience left me shaken.

"I followed proper lock-out procedure, and the machinery moved. What happened?" I asked the supervisor.

"If you disable the robots and the outputs, the dump leaks air and drifts in," he responded.

"Why didn't someone warn me? I could have been killed."

"I forgot," was his response as he hurried away, unconcerned with what had just transpired. This was inexcusable. I put in a call for the safety rep. He never arrived.

UAW international reps were in the plant. Our union asked us if we had any particular safety concerns. I thought this a good time to reach out for help on the lock-out issue with the malfunctioning dump. Several of us wrote our concerns and submitted them to our union. My local union issued me two health and safety forms to fill out, which I did. Some men also sent in concerns. Jack Tolbin received a copy of my safety grievance. I was speaking to Dylan Lukumski when he approached me. He slowly pulled out my letter from an envelope and sneered at me as he held it in his hands.

I looked at the grievance he was staring at and said, "I see you're angry, but if someone had taken my concerns seriously when I first voiced them, I may not have needed to put them in writing. I just want the equipment repaired so no one else risks injury."

Dylan had been unaware of what was taking place until Jack began waving my grievance under his nose. At the time, I was not thinking about the contract negotiations, as I did not participate in plant politics. There were three male electricians who also wrote grievances and were not approached by this management. Health and Safety complaints are strike issues. My local union used me, and I faced the consequences alone.

I had written two Health and Safety grievances without any ulterior motive. Safety was my only motive. The union wanted to use my complaints as bargaining chips although they were not protecting me from GM management's retaliation. An electrician suffered injury on another line with a similar dump, with the same problem. Jack stomped off, taking Dylan Lukumski along with him.

Life began to deteriorate for me after that. I began to watch the lines more and spend less time in Control Support. Eventually, Chad, my harasser, reported to the third shift. He had three years seniority, and replaced me in Control Support. Once again, no one in management would explain the replacement. The atmosphere had definitely changed.

I was moved to E-Zone, where the door frames were made. I had volunteered to work there even though I knew it was considered the worst area for an electrician in the Body Shop to maintain. I needed to get away from the hostile area I had been in. The production people there were good people to work with, which made the job easier. Management thought I would regret going there, but I was having fun learning and didn't realize I was being punished until I questioned my supervisor Bruce. The look that crossed his face when he told me to stay on E-Zone told me everything I needed to know. Adrian was again the production supervisor. I had to deal with his attitude again. He was not a happy camper because he had been doused with 10 gallons of water by some of the guys from the roof. It knocked him to the floor.

December 16 was my birthday. To my great surprise, the workers on E-Zone, production and skilled tradesmen, had a small party for me. It lifted my spirits, but only briefly. During Christmas, I heard my friend Joshua was turning 50. Everyone liked him. When production returned, after the holidays, I mentioned to them that Joshua was going to have a birthday. They loved any excuse to have a party in E-Zone. I bought him a card and circulated it through the Body Shop. I collected 88 signatures on this wonderful man's card. I did not collect money from anyone. Everybody who participated donated their goods out of their own pocket.

The day of the party, I approached his two friends to inform them we were serving the food. As I approached Duncan, his eyes were closed. An inner voice told me to leave him alone. It turned out Duncan was extremely angry that we were throwing Joshua a 50th birthday party, since no one had thrown one for him when he turned fifty. His other friend Bernard walked around rolling his eyes at me and sending disgusted looks my way. They were angry because of the party. Bernard said I had to give every electrician in the Body Shop a birthday party. They reduced me to playing mommy. Duncan tried to spoil Joshua's day. They quit speaking to me and gave me disgusting looks thereafter. No matter what I did, someone always found fault with it.

Bernard said, "If you do it for one, you should do it for all of us."

"That's not my responsibility. I am not your wife, girlfriend, or lover. They have the responsibility for you, not me."

The weekend was approaching. Supervisor Phil Rocha told me, "You are working with Stan this weekend."

"No, I'm not", I said

"Yes, you are."

"If you guys force us to work together after all he's done to me, one of us is going to wind up in a body bag."

I had made up my mind that, if Stan assaulted me, I was going to use my screwdriver or awl on him. I knew this management would assign us to work together and would watch and laugh as Stan terrorized me. When I threatened to defend myself, they thought of how it would look if the public knew.

Our vacation application period was coming upon us in February 2001. As far as vacations were concerned, I had high seniority and knew that receiving my vacation should not be a problem. There were 35 electricians on the midnight shift in the Body Shop at this time. Management was allowing three or four people off at the same time for vacations. There was not a published set of rules locally and, depending on which general foreman you spoke with, the rules changed. I submitted my vacation application February 1, 2001. The application approval period was February 15, 2001 through February 28, 2001.

During this application period, it was deemed that there were too many electricians in the Body Shop on the third shift. Six electricians needed reduction. High seniority had first preference for jobs and shifts. After that, low seniority workers were forced into unwanted positions. The approved vacations were posted and we were free to view them. I was astonished to see my vacation denied. Chad's had been approved for the time I wanted. I protested and called my union steward.

I had 24 years of corporate seniority and Chad had three-and-a-half years. After the six electricians were transferred, the vacations had to be redone. Only two other electricians with higher seniority time were planning vacations, and I knew my vacation should muster approval according to the National Agreement. Skilled Trades abided by the National Agreement for vacations, but again my requested time was denied. The old feelings of despair began. I could feel the nightmare beginning again. Management had refused me my vacation time and approved Chad's. I had 21 years more seniority than Chad.

On March 7, 2001, supervisor, Phil Rocha, approached me. "Did you and Derek have an argument yesterday?" he asked.

"We always argue when he tries to control me. I don't belong to him," I responded.

"Do you know he hurt his hand?"

"No. How bad did he hurt it?"

"He broke it."

I was shocked. I knew the day before, when I was working on a robot crash, Derek had come to see me. He seemed high on something, and I knew he was really angry with me. When he began to ridicule me, I told him to leave my area. I did not ask him to help me with this breakdown. I was quite capable of handling it myself. He watched me with hawk-like eyes the entire time. When I was done he said to me, "The next time you don't kill that other robot, I'm going to have management lay some paperwork on your ass."

"What? You're just mad because I didn't ask you for help. I don't need your help."

He glared hard at me as his eyes darkened. I finished locking the gate and started up the line.

"Get out of my area," I said.

"What?" he asked, amazed.

"Get out. You're acting like you're high on something and I don't need your crap. Get out of my area."

He turned to leave, filled with anger. I returned to my seat. I then heard a hard bang above my head and caught a glimpse of a person rushing around the corner. I got up in time to see Derek smash his plant issued radio to the floor. He was steaming and unhinged. His anger erupted like a volcano and he lost it. Apparently, Derek told supervisor Phil that he hit something instead of me. I later found out he hit the reinforced part of the metal cabinet above where I was sitting, shattering his knuckles. Derek told Phil that he was swinging at me and diverted his punch at the last second into the cabinet. I could have been a one-punch homicide.

I believe Derek felt he could get me to sleep with him by scaring me with violence. He was so high at the time that he only realized how badly he had hurt his hand after the drugs wore off and he could actually feel the pain. Phil wanted me to report to the office and give an account of what happened. When I approached the office, I saw the superintendent, Irvin Casey, Superintendent Gary Sprew, and Phil. Three ranking members of management were present at this meeting. I requested my union steward.

When my union steward arrived, the interview began.

Casey asked, "Are you afraid of Derek?"

I replied, "I have never been afraid of Derek. He would not harm me. I don't know what happened. It's funny how you guys are willing to discharge Derek, but you do nothing to Stan who comes in every day and stalks me.

He has threatened me with physical harm while under the influence of drugs and alcohol. I begged for your help and none of you did a thing. You have the power to stop him, and you still refuse to do so. I believe you enjoy what he is doing."

They looked sheepish and the interview ended without Derek's discharge. I think Derek realized that if he hurt me, he might have to deal with my 250lb husband who played football and tackled people. He knew how to bring down a man. Derek was a really small guy. I asked if Derek would keep his job. He had three kids to support.

The union steward said, "Yes, if Jack Tolbin would stay out of Labor Relations. Jack Tolbin has been to Labor Relations three times to get Derek discharged."

I knew this was not for my benefit. If word spread throughout the plant that I was responsible for Derek's discharge, my life would have been in greater danger. GM management was going to place a big red bulls eye on my back. I never told on anyone. Derek's discharge would spread campus wide and I would become food for the piranhas. As it was, I was anticipating a planned water dump. Jack was willing to discharge Derek over this, but did nothing about my harassment by Stan. Derek was Black and Stan was White. Stan was friends with the managers. How can one effectively manage their old friends? Appropriate action should have been taken against Stan. I was a well skilled Black woman working with all men. Derek deserved some type of discipline, but maybe not a discharge.

A new production supervisor, LeRoy Brown, transferred to my area. Most of the women had problems with him. He was a Black male and tried to dominate us Black females; but he had no electrical experience, so I didn't listen to him. This infuriated him. When I first came to this facility, he was all over me. He ran across the plant floor to see me. He was grinning widely at me and telling me how good my body looked. I managed to keep him at bay and didn't respond to his remarks. The day shift electrician, Gabriel, and I had been talking about a problem the night before. LeRoy was eavesdropping as I suggested that Gabriel call his maintenance supervisor and ask him the question we were discussing. LeRoy, started getting angry.

Anytime a skilled worker asked for their own supervisor, he would get an attitude. We had won the dual supervision rule in the last contract, but management refused to abide by it in Plant 6. If anyone asked LeRoy to straighten out their time clock, issue a pass to medical, authorize a day off, or do anything that required a little work, his response was, "Call your supervisor." Any other time he wanted to be your supervisor. Gabriel came in the next morning to relieve us on the midnight shift. I explained we were having water faults on the robot in the corner on the left side. Gabriel started walking to the right side, the wrong way. I called him back to send him to the left side.

All of a sudden, LeRoy pointed his finger hatefully in my face and yelled. "Let's go."

In disbelief, I asked, "What?"

LeRoy's finger was inches from my face and he said menacingly, "You and me, in the corner right now!"

"Gabriel is on duty now and will handle the problem. It's the end of my shift," I said as I slowly backed away from him.

LeRoy yelled, "You and me are going in that corner right now!"

He was advancing towards me.

I was not going into the dark corner alone with him or with anyone who looked so enraged. I had no idea what he wanted to do to me. Gabriel looked stunned by LeRoy's outburst. I fled in fear before he could vent any more fury.

The man clearly showed his hatred of me and other women. He couldn't help his physical traits, but his volatile demeanor enhanced them and made women afraid of him. He was not a good looking guy at all and women were not attracted to him. He only liked the women he could control by fear and who flattered his ego.

Supervisors slowly controlled women by intimidation, knowing that higher management would not protect the worker against a manager. The supervisors threatened the women with the loss of their jobs if they would not sleep with them. I was not about to let it get to that point, and Leroy chased me all over the Body Shop. I did not respond to his unwanted comments about how good I looked. I was very uneasy about his constant remarks concerning my body. He exhibited some kind of obsession with me. It seemed as if he expected me to smile and giggle like an airhead from his unwanted attention, and he became vicious towards me when I didn't. He could do it because he was an ignorant GM supervisor.

On March 16, 2001, I received my vacation form back. I was entitled to five weeks of vacation time with my corporate seniority. This management approved me for a total of four days of vacation time for the year. They only used the time I had been in Skilled Trades for vacation time. Vacation time is approved by a worker's total time with the company.

When I asked Irvin Casey what happened, he said, "Everyone has more time than you." I knew he had used the trade dates and informed him so. He claimed he had not. Our vacations are approved as follows: 1) Plant seniority date; 2) Corporate seniority; 3) Trade date. My dates are 1-7-85, 10-76, and 12-93 respectively. Irvin had gone straight to the trade date.

I asked, "How does Bernard's full corporate of 1984 and Snead's of 1982 supersede my full corporate of 1976? We all have the same plant date."

He had to think about it. General supervisors seemed to be incompetent in simple vacation approvals. This was the third year in a row in which the vacations were approved incorrectly. Normally, my immediate supervisor approved vacations at my previous facilities. When he realized what he had done, he told me he would redo the vacations and report back to me Monday, March 19, 2001.

Irvin managed to avoid me until Thursday, March 29, 2001.

He said, "If it were up to me I would give you your vacation, but Jack Tolbin said "No."

As he said this, he was smirking, so I knew he had no empathy for me. Everyone knew I had planned a vacation to Las Vegas, where my parents would be meeting us. Management was going to force me to cancel my plans and lose my money to teach me who was boss. I called my union steward. He also sent for my Rights Rep. The Civil Rights Rep was useless. I had asked him several times over the course of things if he was representing management or me. Although he wasn't well educated, he had a nice cushy job, and didn't want to jeopardize it. Management and the union could easily control him. In the beginning, he could not write a proper sentence or spell my name correctly. His final written report read as if it had been written by a Harvard Law School graduate. The spelling and wording were exceptional and this guy couldn't differentiate between their, there and they're.

I was sent to work on the Box-Line, and the Queen paid me a visit. One of the toolmakers was telling her they were surprised to see her on time. She said that she sometimes comes to work on time, but she often needed her beauty sleep. She brought up the subject of vacations. She smiled gleefully as she taunted me, "I received all of my vacation. Didn't you get all of yours?"

My third shift union steward saw me just before my vacation.

He met with me and said, "Just go on vacation and deal with it when you return."

I said, "I don't want to do that and shouldn't have to. I abided by the rules. These people are trying to fire me, and you want me to leave my job up to this union that hasn't helped me yet. I don't think so." This union would tell workers to take their vacation and that the union would fight for their jobs when they returned. I would never trust this union.

"I have a meeting with Irvin Casey at 7 AM. I am sure he will approve your vacation. Stay here until I come back."

My friend Joshua heard him and offered to sit with me. We waited and waited for his return. Finally, Joshua said, "I wonder where he is?"

"He's not coming. He's departed on his own vacation."

"I can't believe he'd do that after just telling you to wait."

"I can."

Joshua had listened to the whole conversation and found it difficult to believe that the union steward had lied to me, but that is exactly what happened. He kept me waiting until he could high-tail it out of the plant without speaking with me. Shortly later I was approached by two fellow male electricians.

"Camille, we need to talk to you."

"About what?"

"Derek is sleeping with the other Camille."

"Nooooo!" I knew everyone would think it was me.

"There's more."

"More what?" I asked, astonished

"He's going around telling all the guys she's freaky."

When I first met Camille Little, she was following LeRoy like a puppy, and he was eating it up. Once Derek slept with her, he controlled her. He would use her to tell me what to do. I witnessed it, myself. She would go see him and ask him what to tell me to do, and then run back to me to tell me what he said because she didn't know what to tell me. They didn't know I could see them. I finally told her to tell him to come see me himself. By using Camille, Derek was indirectly controlling me. He knew I had to do whatever she told me to do. He controlled both female supervisors because he was sleeping with both of them. Both were single, so he was not going after another man's wife. The disgusting part was that they were friends and were sharing the same man. The thought of Derek's hands caressing my body was enough to make me puke; yet he thought he was "stud city" and could sleep with any woman he wanted.

The supervisor, Phil, approached me later that day. I said, "If you hear Derek is sleeping with Camille, it's not this one."

I had been mistaken for the other Camille before. The plant manager held meetings with workers so they could voice their opinions. I was never invited to one, but I heard that the production workers were complaining about Camille. An electrician from the paint department, Lina, said to me, "Camille, what *is* you doing to these people?" Derek explained to her that it was not me, but the supervisor, Camille Little.

After Lina left, Derek said to me, "You know, all you had to do was pretend you didn't know anything and they would have left you alone."

Flabbergasted, I replied, "What kind of Black man are you to tell me to play dumb so that your drugged-out friends can feel better about themselves and superior over me. We have enough issues with people thinking all Blacks are dumb. I would never do something like that. What is wrong with you?"

Derek replied, "My father raised me to be an unassuming Black man."

"Your father did a wonderful job," I shot back.

When my vacation arrived, I took what was contractually mine. Several men had done it before me and after me with no repercussions, and I pointed this out to my civil rights rep. Upon my return, I was immediately placed on disciplinary notice three times. Three different supervisors had placed me on notice over three days. The floor maintenance supervisors honestly did not want to discipline me. There were a handful of supervisors who knew that what was happening was wrong, but they had no choice but to do as they were directed or lose their jobs. They were contract supervisors for various companies that do work for GM and were hoping to get hired by GM. I was transferred, along with another electrician, to the first shift.

There was an argument between the shifts as to who was going to discipline me. I was on notice for over a week, although our local agreement strictly limited this to three days unless an investigation had to be launched.

I questioned my day shift union steward, "Why am I still on notice?"

"They have to investigate."

"What's to investigate? Management knew I took my vacation. In fact, they had counted on it so they could issue me a discipline."

"I agreed with management to keep you on notice."

"Own up to your decision then."

Knowing my local union was a good ol' boy network, I realized I was not going to receive proper representation.

Management and the union agreed that I would be disciplined by third shift. During the interview I asked the supervisor, Bruce, if everyone was being treated the same. He really was at a loss for words. I told him that, since the same superintendent ran the area on all three shifts, the same rules should apply for all shifts. Everyone knew that the Queen could do whatever she wanted without facing any discipline. Bruce became uncomfortable, so I told him to do what he had to do. I knew the harassment was not coming from him, but from Jack Tolbin. I was issued a written reprimand for "absence without reasonable cause." I was happy that I had a background in union negotiations in order to save myself because my union steward was useless during these proceedings. I was stunned by what was happening, but the worst had not even begun.

Or HUMAn Resources Can+ Understand that a noose is inappropriate

89

1 Q. Was it your understanding that she made a complaint at the
2 time she saw the noose?
3 A. I don't recall if it was on the same day or if it was
4 sometime thereafter.
5 Q. All right. So you determined that he didn't follow policy
6 because he didn't notify upper management?
7 A. Correct.
8 MR. ALEXOPOULOS: He said he didn't follow the
9 guideline.
10 THE WITNESS: It's not policy. We have -- a
11 communication protocol would probably be the correct phrase
12 to use.
13 Q. (BY MR. SELINSKY): Didn't follow communication protocol?
14 A. Correct.
15 Q. Do you know why he didn't?
16 A. No. I don't recall why he didn't.
17 Q. Would if I told you that he thought since he didn't see the
18 noose that he didn't have to report it. Does that sound
19 familiar to you?
20 MR. ALEXOPOULOS: Objection. Assumes facts not in
21 evidence.
22 THE WITNESS: I would need to review my notes to be
23 able to refresh my memory on that.
24 Q. (BY MR. SELINSKY): So you have notes on this?
25 A. I have notes of the --

90

1 MR. ALEXOPOULOS: He has them and you have them.
2 MR. SELINSKY: Well, I don't know if I have them all.
3 MR. ALEXOPOULOS: I'm telling you you do.
4 Q. (BY MR. SELINSKY): Let me go back to an underlining issue.
5 You made a determination by notifying upper management and so whether or not he actually
6 notifying upper management and so whether or not he actually
7 sees the noose himself the fact that Ms. Cooper reports it
8 to him, it would have been his obligation to report it to
9 someone higher up; is that correct?
10 A. Correct.
11 Q. Who would he have to report it to?
12 A. The protocol we have in place states that the report can be
13 made to our security. Can be made to Labor Relations'
14 Salaried Personnel. The Medical department. Committee
15 person.
16 Q. Any of those?
17 A. Any -- any of those.
18 Q. Did he ever tell you why he didn't report it?
19 MR. ALEXOPOULOS: Objection. Asked and answered.
20 MR. SELINSKY: Not exactly.
21 THE WITNESS: I would have to.
22 Q. (BY MR. SELINSKY): Look at your notes on that?
23 A. Yeah.
24 Q. And going back to the existence of the noose or not, do you
25 recall whether or not you made a conclusion that there was a

91

1 noose?
2 A. I would have to refer to the notes.
3 Q. If Ms. Cooper actually produced a noose, would that be
4 evidence in your mind that there was one?
5 MR. ALEXOPOULOS: Objection. Calls for speculation.
6 THE WITNESS: I don't know how to answer that
7 question.
8 Q. (BY MR. SELINSKY): Okay. Is presence of a noose at a
9 plant would you consider that a racial threat?
10 MR. ALEXOPOULOS: Objection. Calling for a legal
11 conclusion.
12 THE WITNESS: In our documentation that we use for our
13 training purposes, we do use a noose as an example of
14 something that is considered to be an inappropriate and
15 inappropriate's probably not a strong enough word, but it's
16 not tolerated.
17 Q. (BY MR. SELINSKY): Why isn't it tolerated?
18 A. It can be construed as a racially harassing and also in
19 terms of workplace violence.
20 Q. That the presence of a noose is racially harassing?
21 MR. ALEXOPOULOS: Objection. Calls for a legal
22 conclusion.
23 THE WITNESS: That's not contained in the training
24 materials. What we do state is that a noose is an example
25 of something that is not considered to be appropriate.

92

1 Q. (BY MR. SELINSKY): Well, you said inappropriate's not
2 really strong enough, but what word would you use?
3 A. I would have to refer to the training materials to refresh
4 my memory exactly what is stated in those materials.
5 Q. What is the name of the training materials?
6 A. I don't believe it has a specific title. There's a variety
7 of training materials that are used for the purpose of
8 conducting training regarding those policies.
9 Q. But somewhere in the training materials there's references
10 to nooses?
11 A. Yes. I believe there is.
12 Q. Okay. And you've used those training materials to teach
13 classes or something?
14 A. Yes.
15 Q. Okay. I don't have any other questions for you today.
16 Thank you. Do you have any questions?
17 MR. ALEXOPOULOS: No.
18 (Deposition concluded at 5:35 p.m.)
19
20
21
22
23
24
25

CHAPTER 8

For a while, I was a floater on day shift in the Body Shop until management decided they would use Damon, an ex-manager, in Control Support, and I would take over his job on B-Main. My old supervisor, Corky Russell, became my partner. Every time I had a little robot fault, Corky ran over to instruct me what to do. I tried to think of a way to let him know I didn't need his help, but he was extremely sensitive and needed his ego constantly stroked. He had written a letter to President Bush about how to end the Iraq war, which he insisted on reading to me although I told him I didn't want to hear it. He captured me in my little area and read it to me. When I told him it was a well-written letter his face began to pout. I think he expected me to tell him how smart he was and that President Bush should listen to him. I actually thought he was a sniveling wimp. Corky had a penchant for yelling at me, and I told him several times not to scream at me, but he never screamed at the guys who worked with him. He always retreated from the guys who threatened to knock him on his behind.

When he began to get on my nerves, I finally said, "Corky, it's not necessary for you to come over every time I have a fault. I can handle them. If I run into a problem I can't handle, I'll ask for your assistance. Hopefully, you will be willing to assist me and I will be willing to assist you."

The floor pans, sheets of metal that line the floor of a car or truck, were big, bulky, and heavy, and I wasn't supposed to try lifting them. These were truck floor pans. There were production group leaders who were responsible for problems with the material or heavy lifting of the material. My job was to keep the equipment running smoothly. If weld tips were producing poor welds, if there was equipment failure, needed maintenance of equipment and things of that nature, it was my job to address the issue. Most of the time, if a supervisor was there, he told me what he wanted me to do even if he had no electrical training. Most of the supervisors were unskilled. I had been instructed to do some very dangerous things on the job even though the supervisor had little knowledge about this. I once asked a supervisor what he would do if I became hung up on 480 volts. How would he break my body free to send to my family and not electrocute himself in the process? He stared at me dumbfounded. He didn't have a clue, and he was a maintenance supervisor.

I had been in denial. It finally dawned on me that the situation I was in was reality. I believed that these supervisors were going to go the distance in treating me cruelly. I realized I had to do something to protect myself. It was while I was sitting alone that the idea emerged to write a letter to the heads of the corporation. I used the time while my line was running smoothly to pen my letter. It was obvious to me that Jack and his cronies were about to step up the heat. This shouldn't have happened, MS or not, and I was desperate. I sent letters to corporate heads, the NAACP, and my UAW local Chairman. I needed someone to look out for my interests.

The Queen approached me on B-Main on May 23, 2001 saying, "I heard they switched you with Damon. Do you want to go to Control Support? I can talk to Dylan Lukumski and I'm sure he will send you if I talk to him."

She was smirking the entire time. She enjoyed my discomfort and her hold over management.

All the supervisors catered to her because she would report them to Jack Tolbin. She knew how to use the system and manipulate the male supervisors and they allowed it to happen. It was obvious that most of them had no experience with women in the trades and that I was the first Black female electrician most of them had to interact with. I would have settled for treatment respecting my basic civil rights. The managers also did not understand the role of female competition. She would destroy any female in her path she felt competitive against. The Queen delivered a knockout in round one with her mouth constantly feeding management's ears with things I never said.

On May 24, 2001, I mailed my letters. I was extremely reluctant to send the letter but felt I had no choice. I had reached out to the union and the management for help and I received none. I wanted relief so that my Multiple Sclerosis would not be aggravated. I could feel small flare ups and did not want to experience a major exacerbation. I reported to work every day and did my job plus that of the other electricians who skipped out of work and were at the bar or golf course. In any other plant, I was considered a model employee. Pontiac was strange. If you cheated, used drugs, was intoxicated on the job, used filthy language and yelled at supervisors, you were afforded all the leeway in the world to do what you wanted by this management if you were their friend.

I wrote to many Civil Rights groups and Civil Rights leaders. The NAACP had responded to the KKK incident, which is the reason I had reached out for their help. All the other groups I wrote to during all this ignored my pleas for assistance, which is a travesty for Black America. General Motors executives received my letters but left my fate in the hands of the same people I was complaining about. That is negligence. General Motors executives apparently had no control over plant-level managers and couldn't or wouldn't stop the harassment.

I had taken vacation for two days of the Memorial Day holiday. When I returned on May 30, 2001, management was preparing to write me up for taking my vacation. No one had bothered to check the schedule to see that I was on approved vacation. Upon my return, there was a surprise waiting for me. General Motors had hired S.J. Bashen from Texas to investigate my claims. S. J. Bashen was a Black owned firm. Ordered to Labor Relations by General Foreman, Irvin Casey, he arrived with an arrogant smile. Casey was in a smart aleck mode, and with a smirk said, "Isn't this what you wanted Camille? To talk about all the racism going on around here? Here is your opportunity. Get to Labor."

He seemed to find the situation hilarious. I asked that my union steward be present. I did not think he would adequately represent me, but I would at least have a witness. My UAW Civil Rights rep also showed up. When I first entered the Labor Relations office, two men were in Victor Longella's office with their backs turned to me. They were discussing my letter. Finally, one of the secretaries alerted them to my presence, and one of the men closed the door. He later identified himself as Vincent Breedlove, Corporate Head of Labor Relations for GM. Vincent led me to speak with a Ms. Moss in a reassuring way that they were taking my complaints seriously. As he was leaving, I saw the look of anger on his face directed at me. I then caught him off guard as I asked for his name again. He looked at me strangely and repeated his name.

As soon as I saw Ms. Moss, I knew I must be in the most backwards plant GM had under GM management. Ms. Moss was a gorgeous, dark skinned, articulate Black woman. I believe this management thought I would instantly bond with the sister and pour my heart out to her. As a minority, I knew that this was one of the oldest tricks in the book. It was obvious that this management had no idea of the proper way to deal with minorities. Ms. Moss informed me she worked for GM, although she was independent in her findings. We went through my letter. She was taking names and asking questions. She wanted me to believe she was there for my well-being, but I knew differently. She was there for GM's benefit, since GM was paying her salary. Her company also did investigations for the EEOC. I wondered if the EEOC accepted her report despite the fact that she was being paid by GM. She asked me to be quiet about my letter and not to discuss it. She wanted to know why I had sent a copy to the NAACP. That was a major concern. I told her I needed someone to look out for my interest.

There were only four people in this meeting: Ms. Moss, the Civil Rights rep, Martin Ramirez; the union steward, Leslie Beckman; and myself. We had all agreed to keep this meeting confidential. By the time I returned to my area, a general foreman had told everyone what had taken place. Someone finally silenced him. I decided to give Ms. Moss a chance. On June 5, 2001, an ex- union steward approached me. He said he heard I had written a letter that had management stirred-up. I played dumb.

I pretended not to know what he was talking about; but I knew who had leaked the information. I asked Martin if he had said anything. He replied "NO." I then told him I did not say anything, and I was quite sure Ms. Moss did not say anything, so it must have been my union steward. I told Martin that we had all agreed not to take it out of the Labor office, and that the union steward had no business discussing it in the UAW office. Martin kept trying to defend the union steward. I then contacted our presiding plant union chairman and asked him to zip the union steward's lip. If I had known Martin was going to attend the meeting, I would not have requested my union steward. I did not feel Martin could adequately represent me, but I knew I needed have some sort of union representation. Martin was definitely in over his head. He did not possess the critical thinking skills for this job, nor even the necessary basic English skills.

I also had never worked in a plant where the union and management did not keep a workers business confidential. Ms. Moss left, returned to Texas and left me there alone. The managers and union circled me like hungry wolves. I couldn't believe that the vice-presidents sitting in the GM building had left my fate in the hands of the people I was complaining about. The wolves pounced, feasting with frenzied hunger as they tore away, determined to devour me.

On June 7, 2001, Martin Ramirez visited me. He told me that Victor Longella claimed he had made an agreement with the general foreman, Heath, to arrange a meeting between Stan and me. He later came out to see me personally and I told him everything was okay. Victor stated that I must not remember our conversation because of my MS. Nothing made sense. Drugged, volatile and liquor-influenced men were terrorizing me and I failed to remember this conversation, because of my MS! I had gone to Labor because no one in the Body Shop would help me. The meeting never transpired. There was no need to conduct a meeting between Stan and me. All General Motors had to do was to tell Stan to quit threatening me or face the loss of his job. GM had the power to do so. Because of the alcohol I smelled on Mr. Longella's breath, I believe it's more than likely that he did not remember.

Ramirez told me that Jack Tolbin had admitted to canceling my class. The other man was allowed to perform the job, without training and I should have been afforded the same opportunity. Instead management transferred me back to the line.

On June 8, 2001 I received another visit from Martin.

He said, "Jack Tolbin removed you from Controls because you have Multiple Sclerosis. He needs a sharp thinker. Because you have asked five people not to talk in your ear at the same time while you're trying to concentrate, he can't use you." All the electricians say the same thing including the queen. We had SAFETY concerns. "Pay attention to what you are doing." We are trying to do the job effectively and not get injured in the process.

He removed me from another coveted job because he is so concerned about my Multiple Sclerosis, yet he never intervened while I was suffering abuse by his friends and I begged for help. He had been a friend of my number one harasser, Stan, since 1985 when Jack first came to work for GM. Jack's explanation was without merit because I could work all 19 lines in Body Shop. Most of their "stars," including the queen, could only work one or two lines. Instead of building better workers to become assets to the company, these leaders seemed to want to break you down.

On June 19th, 2001, Martin Ramirez returned to see me offering a different excuse from Jack. This time Jack said he'd had a conversation with me two years earlier in which I expressed cognitive concerns to him about my MS, so he took me off Control Support. The conversation never happened. I had been doing controls for eight weeks before he took me off.

In truth, he was very angry about the Health and Safety complaints I had written. Jack told Martin in April 2001, that he vaguely knew me. He vaguely knew me in April, but he now somehow remembered a conversation in which I emotionally voiced my concerns to him about my MS. I have never shed a tear because I have MS, and I would seek male emotional support only from my husband. Everyone knew I had MS. It's in my plant medical file since I had been on medical leave twice for it. I left educational material around, and anyone who had a loved one afflicted with this debilitating disease could feel free to come and talk about it with me. I also provided my phone number for people to call.

Several days later, a tour was coming through the plant. My maintenance supervisor was a young man by the name of Seth Ballard. I worked in an isolated area, had been on this line only five weeks, and was the latest addition to the area. Some of the guys had been on this line for years. There was junk and garbage all around. I kept my small area clean. Seth ordered me to clean up the area after the men.

I said, "Seth, I just arrived in this area. Have the guys clean up after themselves. I am not the maid." Seth was a 22 year old fresh out of the military.

I continued to keep my little area clean. I asked the guys if they had been ordered to clean up and was informed that the third shift supervisor was doing the cleaning.

The next day Seth returned and said sarcastically, "You did a real bang up job of cleaning the area."

I replied, "Seth, I am not the maid. Why are you forcing me, the only woman, to clean up behind the men? I am an electrician just like the guys, not the maid."

Unbeknownst to me, the electrician pranksters in the Body Shop had stolen Seth's plant vehicle. He was angry about it because he had to walk.

He towered over me and shouted, "I want this area five-sd by the end of the day or I will discipline you." I had no clue what he meant.

I asked, "What does that mean?"

He yelled while turning red, "A place for everything and everything in its place." It was military language. I again told him I was not the maid.

"This is years of accumulating junk that the guys brought here. I do not know what some of the stuff is. It's the millwrights', pipefitters', and other tradesmen's garbage."

"I am issuing you a direct order to clean it up or I will discipline you."

I could not believe it and called for my union steward to write a grievance for gender discrimination. He did not want to write it, but reluctantly he did. My union steward and I had clashed previously regarding overtime hours charged incorrectly to me. I had asked my supervisor, Seth, to straighten out the discrepancy. Apparently, he took the easy way out and sent for my union steward, Leslie. Leslie approached me angrily about coming on this call.

He yelled at me, "How many hours were you fucked out of?"

Shocked by his language I said, "Excuse me?"

"How many hours were you fucked out of?"

"Hold it. You have no right speaking to me like that. You have never heard me speak like that and I don't appreciate you talking to me like that."

"I am tired of coming out on fucking calls that are management's fucking responsibility."

"I did not call you. Seth did. Go curse at Seth."

"I will write your fucking grievance."

"No, you need to leave my area now."

I was upset that he would address me in that manner and walked over to visit my friend Shawn. I could hear everything that happened on my line while talking to him, our lines were connected. My union steward rounded the corner smiling at Shawn like the Cheshire Cat. Shawn was a very big guy and the union steward did not have the guts to speak to him the way he had spoken to me. Once he spotted me, he offered a weak apology for his inexcusable behavior.

I began experiencing problems with my thyroid in 20001. My doctor was trying to regulate it, but to no avail. I would have to undergo radioactive iodine treatment. Since I would be radioactive and to take special precautions to protect others, especially pregnant women, I took two sick days off. When I returned, Seth demanded my doctor's excuse. We were required to have a doctor's excuse for any absence to avoid a reprimand. If you left work an hour early because of the flu, management could demand that you see your doctor and get a written excuse.

I handed it to the supervisor and he said, "I'm going to call him right now."

"My doctor can't discuss my medical condition with you."

"We'll see about that." He left in a huff, still upset about the grievance I had written against him.

He returned and said, "I can't believe you wrote this grievance against me."

"Seth, once a grievance has been reduced to writing you can no longer speak with me about it without my union steward present." We had already verbally discussed the situation.

We were isolated and he was turning red. I did not want to experience his fury. He said, "An employee should do whatever a supervisor tells him, without question. That's how we did it in the military."

"I am a civilian. We have a contract and GM claims they are an Equal Opportunity Employer."

Thankfully, at this point, another supervisor, Brandon, walked up. I liked Brandon. He tried to treat me fairly. I asked Brandon to explain to Seth that once a grievance was made in-writing he could no longer speak with me about it. I had followed proper union grievance procedures by trying to work it out with the supervisor first.

Camille McMillan
Oak Park, MI 48237

May 18, 2001

Gerald A. Knechtel, Vice President
General Motors Corporation
General Motors Building
3044 West Grand Boulevard
Detroit, MI 48202

Dear Mr. Knechtel:

I am a black female, journeyman electrician working in the Body Shop at Pontiac East Assembly (PEA). I am compelled to send this letter because of the negative working conditions that I am forced to endure with minute support. I hope the letter generated on November 14, 1997, by Mr. Gerald A. Knechtel to WDIV-TV (Detroit, Michigan – Channel 4) is genuinely sincere. There are many injustices occurring at PEA; internally, I have spoken with numerous employees in "position of authority" with unsatisfactory results. This document is not intended for litigation purposes, but to give insight to the negative environment at PEA. Managers in the Body Shop are continuously placing the "Corporation" in legal jeopardy without considering the ramifications of their actions. The following in an indication of incidents that have transpired in the Body Shop, and I have more incidents documented.

For two years I was assigned to the same area. There were also five friends who were in the same area. On November 29, 1999, there was a confrontation about the location of my toolbox. I had previously been ordered by man #1 to move my toolbox, because man #2 wanted my space. My toolbox had occupied the space for almost a year, and with our limited amount of space, I had no where to relocate without infringing on the rights of others. As a result, I refused to move my toolbox.

During my absence over the holiday weekend (during this same period), my toolbox was moved into someone else's space. Subsequently, I had it returned to it's original spot. Man #1, waited for my male coworker, who had assisted me in moving the toolbox, leave the area. After my coworker left, Man #1 then proceeded to verbally assault me, and then he stormed-off. Man #2, who worked the midnight shift, arrived in the area at approximately 09:30 p.m. During this time frame, I was having a conversation with my supervisor, ████████ Man #2 rushed into the area, glanced at my supervisor, and then proceeded to scream at me. Man #2 appeared to be very inebriated as he ignored the fact that I was engaged in a conversation with my

I

117

supervisor, and he did not seem to care that a member of the management staff was present and observing his behavior.

To my dismay, however, my supervisor exited the scene very swiftly and left me with this enraged intoxicated, volatile man. Man #2 became verbally abusive as he blocked my exit, and threatened me. He then proceeded to push my toolbox into the aisle-way, totally disregarding the forklift traffic. I approached the General Foreman, ████████ to alert him about the scene that had just taken placed. Mr. ████ course of action was to make Man #2 return my toolbox to its proper place, even though you could distinctly smell alcohol on Man #2's breath.

From that point on, I have been subjected to threatening gestures, glares and stares, and having my workspace violated. For example, on December 3, 1999, I was at my toolbox with another coworker. I was having problems with my key working, because for some reason it would not fit the lock. While I checked to see if I had the correct key, my coworker checked my lock. As it would turn out, my locks had been glued; *my personal property had been violated*. As a result of my locks being glued I had to have the maintenance supervisor call the millwright to cut the locks off.

I began to fear for my safety and I sought resolution from Labor Relations. I conferred with the Labor Relations representative ████████. I informed him that I only wanted to have the harassment ceased. Since I have Multiple Sclerosis, it was imperative to bring closure to this harassment. I emphasized the fact that my body could not endure the undo stress that was being put on me, and I certainly could not withstand a physical assault. Having MS and being harassed consistently would cause my body to plummet in an exacerbation of my illness, which I may, not every recover from. Instead of relief from the harassment, it was intensified!

On January 18, 2000, I reported to work at approximately 11:00 a.m. Several other electricians informed me of the latest incident. A picture of "road kill" was posted in my area; my name was on it with a very negative caption beside it. These electricians were appalled that the harassment had not abated. I made countless pleads to "management" to take corrective action. My pleas were ignored and the harassment continued until the NAACP became involved in the KKK episode. Only after this investigation did the harassment toward me dwindle.

These incidents pose some serious questions that have not been addressed properly. For example:

1. Why were my tormentors not prohibited from this behavior? Does not "**NO**" mean "**NO**" in any form? Asking for my harassment to be **STOPPED** is saying "**NO**" to negative behavior that was inflicted upon me.
2. Why didn't and/or couldn't the Shop Floor supervisors and General Foremen intervene?
3. After I expressed by terror to the Labor Relation Representative, ████████, why did he not take any action?

4. ████████is superintendent of Maintenance for all shifts in the Body Shop. Mr. ████ knows Man #2 well; why didn't ████ell put an end to it?
5. Why was I left in a "Hostile Work Environment" despite my pleas for help?
6. Are these not serious examples of my being harassed?

These are interesting questions when you consider the fact that there are no "*secrets*" in the Body Shop. So again, I must ask, why wasn't something done? I had informed management on all of the shifts; I followed proper protocol. As far as ███████████ is concerned, he has never spoken to me again.

Unfortunately, hidden racism and gender related harassment has continued to be a problem for me. Jobs were promised to me that never materialized. The Infrared Class, I was to attend, was cancelled a week before I was slated to attend. Possibly, this was legitimate, but management had a white male slated for that position. I was also promised a Controls job by General Foreman, ███████████, that never materialized. How strange that I was replaced when one of my former harassers was bumped to the third shift. Joe never explained why I was replaced.

There is a strong need for a valid and uncontestable vacation time off policy; everything is decided by ████████. With 25 years seniority this year, I was denied vacation, again, because the incorrect eligibility date was used. I abided by the contract for submission of time off and was in line of seniority. After I had informed the Union of concerns, my form was submitted 02/02/01, we were blocked from viewing the schedule and it was removed on March 30, 2001. With manpower very close in numbers, per shift, Dean Bell had different rules for each shift.

After the General Foreman had redone the vacations, he told me I was still denied, per ███████ ████ decided only two electricians on the midnight shift could go on vacation at any given time, and I was number three. The other shifts were allowed three of four people off at a time. ████████ also included the Infrared Electrician, who never maintains a line, in his count.

On March 29, 01, I was denied vacation. I was informed that it was pe████████. With all of my money invested in my vacation and none of it refundable, I had no choice but to go. Upon my return, I was penalized; however, white males who have done this before me were not. We can no longer determine if vacations are based on the contract or on biases.

Fair treatment is not applied across the board. There is a white female electrician who receives special treatment. She comes in late and boasts about it, informed me she had received all of her vacation approval, works her own schedule and then gets all of the over time she wants in violation of the 71 sheet. She is also on the *Suggestion Committee* and management made sure that she was trained as a specialist. Management exhibits flagrant favoritism where she is concerned. She has informed me that her friend, General Foreman ████████████, password protected the vacation

3

schedules. We were always allowed previously to view same schedule. She is privileged to many management decisions

As I stated earlier, I do not intend to litigate, at this time. I do not seek special treatment, even though I have seen Management give special treatment to white males and females that have injured themselves *off* the job. However, I do seek fair and equal treatment. Although I have a debilitating disease, no one has tried to make my situation better. Management, as I have duly noted in this communication, would not even step in to keep me from being harassed.

In conclusion, if General Motors is serious about their sexual harassment and diversity commitment, someone needs to inform Pontiac East. What has happened to me, should never have happened. It is still hard to believe that GM managers allowed this. I ask that managers take action when incidents are brought to their attention. Situations that make the news are not being corrected, here. Instead, they are being swept under the rug. In case of retaliation from management, here, I am sending a copy of this letter to the NAACP. I do not want this letter in the paper, nor any other media, nor do I seek publicity as a result of this letter. This situation has already taken a toll on my health! The bottom line is that I seek fairness for all.

Sincerely,

Camille F. McMillan

Cc: Guy Briggs, Vice President
General Motors

Gary L. Cowger, Vice President
General Motors, Labor Relations

Dr. Eugene Rogers, President
NAACP, North Oakland

Rev. Wendell Anthony, President
NAACP, Detroit

Bill King, UAW Local 594
Plant Chairman

Files

4

SENDER: COMPLETE THIS SECTION

- Complete items 1, 2, and 3. Also complete item 4 if Restricted Delivery is desired.
- Print your name and address on the reverse so that we can return the card to you.
- Attach this card to the back of the mailpiece, or on the front if space permits.

1. Article Addressed to:

Mr. Gary L. Cowger
Vice Pres. General Motors
300 Renaissance Center
Detroit, MI 48265

COMPLETE THIS SECTION ON DELIVERY

A. Received by (Please Print Clearly) | B. Date of Delivery
Woodson

C. Signature
X William Woodson
☐ Agent
☐ Addressee

D. Is delivery address different from item 1? ☐ Yes
If YES, enter delivery address below: ☐ No

3. Service Type
☒ Certified Mail   ☐ Express Mail
☐ Registered   ☐ Return Receipt for Merchandise
☐ Insured Mail   ☐ C.O.D.

4. Restricted Delivery? (Extra Fee)   ☐ Yes

2. Article Number (Copy from service label)

PS Form 3811, July 1999   Domestic Return Receipt   102595-99-M-

---

...MPLETE THIS SECTION

- ...items 1, 2, and 3. Also complete item 4 if Restricted Delivery is desired.
- Print your name and address on the reverse so that we can return the card to you.
- Attach this card to the back of the mailpiece, or on the front if space permits.

1. Article Addressed to:

Mr. Guy Briggs
Vice Pres. General Motors
300 Renaissance Center
Detroit, MI 48265

COMPLETE THIS SECTION ON DELIVERY

A. Received by (Please Print Clearly) | B. Date of Delivery
Woodson

C. Signature
X William Woodson
☐ Agent
☐ Addressee

D. Is delivery address different from item 1? ☐ Yes
If YES, enter delivery address below: ☐ No

3. Service Type
☒ Certified Mail   ☐ Express Mail
☐ Registered   ☐ Return Receipt for Merchandise
☐ Insured Mail   ☐ C.O.D.

4. Restricted Delivery? (Extra Fee)   ☐ Yes

2. Article Number (Copy from service label)

PS Form 3811, July 1999   Domestic Return Receipt   102595-99-M-

---

SENDER: COM... SECTION

- Complete items 1, 2 and 3. Also complete item 4 if Restricted Delivery is desired.
- Print your name and address on the reverse so that we can return the card to you.
- Attach this card to the back of the mailpiece, or on the front if space permits.

1. Article Addressed to:

Mr. Gerald A Knechtel
VICE PRES. General Motors
300 Renaissance Center
Detroit, MI 48265

COMPLETE THIS SECTION ON DELIVERY

A. Received by (Please Print Clearly) | B. Date of Delivery
Woodson

C. Signature
X William Woodson
☐ Agent
☐ Addressee

D. Is delivery address different from item 1? ☐ Yes
If YES, enter delivery address below: ☐ No

3. Service Type
☒ Certified Mail   ☐ Express Mail
☐ Registered   ☐ Return Receipt for Merchandise
☐ Insured Mail   ☐ C.O.D.

4. Restricted Delivery? (Extra Fee)   ☐ Yes

(Copy from service label)

July 1999   Domestic Return Receipt   102595-99-M-1789

CHAPTER 9

On July 26, 2001, I was summoned to Labor Relations, with Darren Byram and Vincent Breedlove as the Labor Reps. Martin Ramirez came to represent me. Breedlove informed me that they did not want to talk about the "Roadkill" picture or anything concerning the harassment with Stan Minard and the threats on my life, the ADA act violations or the gender harassment after Thanksgiving in 1999. The sexual harassment by Derek was slowly brewing and there was nothing I could do. The only thing they wanted to discuss was the vacation schedule and GM's plan for diversity. They did not want to discuss the harassment by Stan.

They were trying to implement a new vacation procedure against the vacation policy negotiated in the 1999 contract talks between the International UAW and General Motors. It ensured vacation by corporate seniority and not favoritism. Darren Byram stated that it would take a while to change attitudes. They asked me about S. J. Bashen's response time. I responded that they were very slow. Byram said that it was because S. J. Bashen was a new company out of Texas and GM was not used to working with them. GM and my union refused to provide me a copy of the report. Everything was verbal. Later when I got my civil case file in 2006 I found a letter in my legal file written by a member of management stating that

S. J. Bashen advised GM not to act on my concerns because the statute of limitations had run out and it was too late for me to do anything.

They tried to intimidate me into saying they had alleviated all of my concerns. These two men were staring at me with hard eyes as they harshly asked me questions and I was alone.

Byram said, "Can we get you to say we have addressed you concerns?" and I refused.

When I asked about the jobs Jack had taken from me, Vincent Breedlove said with a sly smile, "We're working on that."

Labor was going to consider my case closed until Martin Ramirez reminded them of Jack Tolbin's statement concerning my MS and his ADA violation. Jack admitted that he violated ADA rules. Ramirez told me that Vincent Breedlove had said that he was trying to ""undermine the company" by informing me of what Jack Tolbin had said concerning my Multiple Sclerosis. Ramirez was extremely nervous and said he would not tell me what else Vincent had said.

Martin Ramirez was my UAW Civil Rights Rep, and his job was to protect me. He withdrew my gender discrimination charge against Seth without my approval. He wanted me to write the grievance against Jack Tolbin for discrimination concerning my MS. I did not want him to handle that. I felt he would have immediately settled it in the company's favor. The grievance I wrote against Seth was a good grievance, but my union did not want to pursue it. I found later in my civil suit file a signed, time recorded, and dated document in which Vincent Breedlove threatened to fire a union rep if the union attempted to help me. This plant did as they wanted. GM management or Federal laws were not followed. If they wanted to fire you, they fired you.

On August 9, 2001, I was sitting in my work area at lunch. Derek had come to visit me. Jack Tolbin came over and demanded to speak to me in private. I could do nothing but walk with him to this isolated area. He ordered me to a meeting with Labor Relations. I headed up to the Labor Relations department. Once I arrived, Ramirez also arrived and said that management was planning to give me their answer to Jack's discriminatory remark.

I asked, "Why should I waste my time to sit through more lies? Tell them to put it in writing." I asked Ramirez for a copy of his investigation and returned to my job.

After the meeting Ramirez came back to see me. He stated that Vincent Breedlove claimed he had investigated thoroughly why Jack took me off Control Support and "because of my conversation with Jack Tolbin" (which never occurred) concerning my MS two years earlier. GM managers seemed to believe that those afflicted with MS were dumb individuals and we couldn't think. Jack had taken me off the job I had been doing for about eight 8 weeks. Labor said general foreman, Dylan Lukumski, a ranking member of management, had no right to give me this job, although he had given it to others. More lies were constructed to twist the situation. I was also due to go on vacation the following week and the timing was to give me something to think about over vacation.

The following week my family visited Washington D.C. My daughter was able to see what our country was supposed to stand for and that justice was supposed to be a right for all Americans. I was naive and once believed it. The Pontiac Truck plant taught me differently.

An electrician, Hans, came to see me, visibly upset. He had been upstairs working when another employee arrived for work. This employee was angry that his overtime was cut off in accordance with the rules of the contract and he was venting his rage. The contract stated that low overtime hours get the overtime first and he had high overtime hours. He was a known racist, and I was the easiest target. Apparently he called me a "Black nigger bitch" in front of two employees and a GM supervisor. I wasn't there but Hans said he reported it to Labor and was told, "You should be ashamed of yourself coming in here and making false allegations against a fellow employee." This man's wife had a corporate job with GM. The upset employee would take her access code into the employee time and change the times of work for his buddies.

On September 5, 2001, Irvin Casey came to see me at 1:10 PM. He offered me the Infrared position again. He explained that they were adding another person to Infrared and wanted to know if I was still interested in the job. At 2:05 PM, Martin Ramirez showed up with a copy of his report. I believe they thought that I would withdraw charges against GM if they gave me the Infrared job. Martin omitted the last page of his report. I discovered there was one more page which he had written that no discrimination was found, but he refused to turn over that last page to me. Another union official saw it and told me but he was also scared to give me a copy.

On September 11, 2001 our nation was struck by terror. I watched as Americans of almost all races, religions, genders creeds and colors banded together for America's sake. It was a time of tragedy for our nation but, as a country, we pulled together. Although my situation affected my everyday life, we were all in mourning and concentrated on helping and protecting our nation. Drills were instituted all over the country to try to protect us. I tried to push my situation aside, although it was very troublesome for me while mourning for our fellow Americans.

In October 2001, I finally received the proper Infrared training along with two other men who were permitted to do the job while I'd been removed. At the end of the training we were administered a fifty-question test. In order to become certified, one had to pass the test with at least a 70%. In addition, we had to complete a homework assignment and mail it back for grading within thirty days. Upon completing these requirements, one would receive a certification from Flir Infrared as a Level I Thermographer.

I was working in the Infrared office when I realized that one of the men had received his initial certificate for completing the class, and I had never received mine. Our main Thermographer, Prince, went searching for mine with the union, but he did not find it. I was not surprised and said to Prince, "It will probably show up tomorrow." Prince was a good man. He would tell you in a minute he only had a ninth grade education. When I arrived home after work, I called Flir Infrared. A very pleasant woman by the name of Rita took my call, complimented me on the homework assignment, and informed me I had scored 92 % on the test and she had mailed my certificate to my union leaders. She said she would call the union rep. herself. I asked that my certificate and all future mailings be sent directly to my home. The following day, behold, my certificate mysteriously appeared.

On October 24, 2001, I walked to the canteen area to refill my water cup with ice. As I glanced across the aisle, I saw the young supervisor, Reed Small, trying to do the electrician's job. His department electrician was sitting there reading the paper and smoking. Reed glanced over at me as I was going to get ice. On my way back, Reed crossed the aisle, approached me, and said, "I can't get Ryan off his ass to do his job so the next time I'll just come and get you." I told Reed I had a line to maintain and did not appreciate the fact that he was scared of his male electrician and would venture over to make me do his job.

I saw general supervisor Irvin Casey and explained the situation. Irvin responded, "In an emergency situation, Reed is within his rights to order you to do the job."

I said, "Irvin, this was no emergency. Reed's man is in the department and Reed is scared to address him but not afraid to address me." I knew it was useless to continue talking to Irvin Casey. Irvin was a master at twisting a situation around rather than dealing with it. I received no help from anyone from GM, so I went to see Mr. H. Wallace Parker, attorney at law. He took my case along with 14 other cases of discrimination from this plant.

On Dec 17, 2001, one of the other minority women in the suit told me that she had been summoned to Labor Relations a few days earlier. She'd been accused of spreading rumors about a supervisor and another new graduated female electrician. Both were married. She told me that Darren Byram, of labor relations, said that I had come in to see him and complained that she was starting rumors on another woman having an affair. This never happened. Yes, there were plenty of rumors circulating about the supervisor and this electrician's behavior, but I didn't care. I'm not the moral police of the plant. I only have control of myself.

The GM attorney asked me during my deposition if I ever asked the labor rep if he had accused me of accusing this employee of starting rumors. Why would I talk to a man who never helped me when I previously begged for help? I did not need more lies. I also would not entertain petty gossip with this management. Gossip is normal in the plants, and has been at all three plants that I worked at. The Pontiac Truck managers however disciplined petty gossipers, but allowed volatile, alcoholic, drug-influenced employees to terrorize women and people with disabilities. It was my opinion that this labor rep was trying to instigate an altercation between the other woman and me. That way they could fire us both and possibly end these lawsuits. I just stayed away from her. I did not need to deal with anyone so easily manipulated. I stood alone in this. My union was corrupt and useless.

CHAPTER 10

The holidays were approaching. I had requested to take off the day after New Year's Day. I had submitted the paperwork in accordance with our National Agreement and was denied the time off by general foreman Dylan Lukumski. When I reported to work after the holidays, the queen was not in. I called for my union steward. The queen and a white male were granted the time off even though I had applied for it first and had more earned vacation time than the White male. The vacation application period based on seniority, was over and it was first-come first-served. I had submitted for the time before the queen and the White male. They were granted the time and I was once again denied.

In February, 2002 I again submitted my vacation request in accordance with our National Agreement. I had grieved the new vacation procedure that management had tried to implement against the National Agreement. The International Union had sent a rep to settle the dispute, and the dispute about vacation time which was once again settled in my favor. When I received my vacation approval, I realized immediately that my right had been violated. Amos Horace had refused the vacation that was due to me. I tried to talk with him about it but he would not listen. I then had to write a "bargaining in bad faith" grievance, which was once again settled in my favor.

Amos was not happy. He hated anyone who would challenge him, especially a woman. He had been arrested at the plant for assault on an elderly female in his family. The guys told me he had duct-taped the woman's mouth and assaulted her. One electrician carried a piece of duct tape and covered his mouth with it every time he passed Amos. Amos said nothing to this man, but he went after any woman who challenged his word. LeRoy Jones had helped to get him out of jail, the electricians told me. GM knew Amos had a volatile history with women, especially since his arrest was during working hours on GM property.

Shortly after this, I heard that the queen had been diagnosed with MS. Management was upset. The queen wanted to speak with me personally. Only Damon had the courage to ask me to speak with her. I said I would help her through this regardless of how she treated me. Management arranged for someone to cover my area while I sat with the queen for well over an hour while she explained her symptoms. I had experienced many of them myself. She informed me she was having memory problems. She had a line down four hours because of her memory. Management seemed happy I was talking to her.

March 15, 2002, a suit was filed by attorney H. Wallace Parker against GM alleging discrimination at Michigan's Oakland County Circuit Court.. The Honorable John J. McDonald decertified the class action status, and we each filed our separate claims. After filing the lawsuit, I did not discuss it with co-workers. General foreman, Amos Horace, approached me several times wanting to find out what I knew. I played dumb. Amos also encouraged me to file suit against Jack Tolbin with the Michigan Department of Civil Rights for disparity treatment. I was working when he approached me. I had just finished a job on another plaintiff's line. He saw me there and rushed over. I switched the line back on, turned around and there he stood.

"How you doing?" he asked.

Mistrustfully, I said, "I'll live."

"There's a way for you to stop Jack."

"Really?" was all I could manage to say.

"Go to the Michigan Department of Civil Rights and file charges on him."

I choked on my own air but managed to say, "Okay?" as if totally interested. He bought my interest and continued.

"File charges against him for disparity treatment. He makes a difference in how he treats you and the queen because of race. He can't do that."

I backed up saying in my best "air-headed" voice, "Okaaay, thank you Amos. Thank you."

He walked away, smugly thinking he had planted a seed in my mind to do his bidding.

I knew he wanted Jack's job as superintendent and was trying to use me to do his dirty work. He seemed to think that if Jack was fired, he would get the job. I was surprised and appalled by his actions and continued to play dumb.

According to our local agreement, the rules of overtime changed. We were no longer under the full utilization agreement. "Full utilization" means that everyone in Skilled Trades is allowed to work overtime. We were to work overtime according to our overtime hours. People with low overtime hours worked the overtime first. Managers in the body shop decided that certain electricians were no longer qualified to work on the weekends and holidays. I became one of them. I could work these jobs all during week, but on the weekends, I was considered unqualified". The queen was afforded all the overtime she wished. Apparently, GM had trained unqualified electricians and new work rules were always cropping up. Many of these rules were against our negotiated National Agreement contract. The people who had been in "Control Support" were always qualified. Dylan Lukumski also approached me. He said that management was adding on a new classification called "Weamer". He made it sound like a wonderful opportunity to give up my electrician classification and become a Weamer. I guess he didn't know that I knew that Weamers were only in certain plants and I would have to move if I switched my classification. Weamers only take care of robots. I was shocked that his morals had sunk so low that he was really ready to ruin my life. I would never give up my electrician status.

With the new rule of being qualified, supervisors would choose the employees they wanted to work, affecting the incomes of the newly unqualified electricians. If management liked you, you were deemed "qualified", if they didn't like you then you were deemed "unqualified". In doing so, acts of overt discrimination began. Since I'd been removed from the job of Control Support, I was not "qualified" to work in the body shop on the weekends, even though I could run all the lines in the body shop during the week. The queen was not very proficient at running the lines. Her skills were in operating the robot, in which management had provided her exclusive one-on-one training with the experts. Not only was I not qualified according to management, but they began kicking me out of the Body Shop on the weekends and giving me more strenuous physical jobs. Nothing made sense.

I was in the general assembly and trim areas one weekend they needed me to work and I noticed something strange. Everywhere I worked, it seemed I saw Stan Minard. We would have different assignments, but he always found me. He would grab an in-plant vehicle and follow me around to my job assignments, parking and staring at me with hate. At first, I thought I was just imagining this until I saw him around my work area five times in one day. Once again, I began to fear for my life and safety, and grabbed my awl to defend myself. My fear increased as he circled me like a vulture. I knew management would not help me out, but I did have numerous tools to use as weapons

I was talking to my friend Shawn after Stan stalked me all day. Stan saw me, placed himself in my field of vision and began to give me menacing looks.

I asked Shawn, "Please turn slowly to your right and see Stan."

Shawn said, "Ummm."

Stan was so busy menacing me with his eyes he never realized Shawn was watching him. When Stan finally realized he was being observed, he hastily turned away in anger. I sent a letter to my attorneys in case something happened to me. I wanted them to know that Stan was stalking me again.

During Christmas shutdown in 2002, I was in my assigned area waiting for instructions. I had been there for more than two hours, and not one supervisor had come around. I walked to the front of the plant for a minute, bypassing my area manager. When I returned, supervisor Chip threatened me with a write-up. He claimed he had been looking for me for over two hours and had not seen me. That was an outright lie and I told him so.

I also asked him, "Are you Jack's new hit man?"

Chip said, "I do not appreciate the comment."

I responded, "I don't appreciate your willingness to write me up when I was in my area all morning. You never came near my area. I have been working unsupervised all morning and when I take a break, you want to write me up."

I had been working in the Infrared department when we acquired two cameras. Prince would go out on a special route and I would cover his area of responsibility. Prince would cover more difficult areas to use Infrared since he was a higher level Thermographer. We worked like this for several months. A newly graduated apprentice was assigned to my old work area. The supervisor, Phil Rocha, asked me to give the new guy a hand. The line went down and it was time to change weld caps. I told the new electrician that I would take care of the line and he could change caps. I had one final procedure to do, when my partner Corky sprinted over from the other side trying to take charge of the breakdown. He never asked me a thing.

Corky proceeded to the flex system and started inputting information. The flex system held information to run the line. He was trying to impress the new guy, with his knowledge, and totally screwed up the line. I had the information he wanted up on my computer, but he was not skilled enough in that area to see it.

He started screaming at me, "You have what I need up on your computer. Why didn't you tell me?"

I said, "Quit screaming at me. I didn't know what you wanted. You have your own computer and should have been able to look it up. Besides, you never asked me a thing and charged over here to show off for the new guy. Now that you screwed up the breakdown, you're embarrassed and want to take it out on me."

I called my union steward first to give the union a chance to diffuse the situation. I still had a little faith that the union would step up to the plate. Corky was always screaming at the managers and me. He was upset about his treatment on supervision and would constantly try to take it out on me.

The Union steward told management to inform Corky to stop yelling at me. We were down 45 minutes on this unnecessary breakdown. I had been first on the job, and when support came out no one would listen to what I had to say or ask me questions concerning the breakdown.

I was watching a line in the floor pan area. LeRoy Brown was the production supervisor. LeRoy started following me on every job and watching me like a hawk. After the incident about going in the corner with him, I had managed to avoid him. There were complaints about him from other women, and management transferred him to my area. Although I was a Skilled Tradesman and had a different supervisor, he knew he could get by with harassing me and I would receive no help.

First LeRoy tried to flatter me, telling me how good I looked and saying that because we were both Black our relationship should be different. When he could not get through with flattery, he became nasty. This is how sexual abuse begins in the plant. The supervisors begin sweet talking and try to flatter a woman. When the woman fails to respond in the manner they desire, they become hardened. The employee's job is in their hands now, they use that leverage against the employee. Many women have gone through it. I told LeRoy that his comments about my body made me uncomfortable and were inappropriate.

In every supervisor's office, there is a computer with the body shop Zones on it. When a line goes down, that particular area on the computer screen turns red. It normally registers on the computer before it registers on the marquee. LeRoy, sat in his office and waited. As soon as he saw my line registering red, he flew from his office to beat me to the job. I was standing on the bridge one day and he did not see me. The alarm then went off to summon me and he flew out of the office. He was waiting for me on the job when I got there. He began to give me hateful stares.

A day later, a robot was malfunctioning and the bank was low on floor pans. My supervisor asked me if I wanted to shut it down to try to find the problem. I told her I would keep the line flowing until we acquired a "bank" which is a full amount of built doors ready to use. I kept the robot teach pendant which controls the robot manually in my reach so that I could reset the faults. LeRoy continued to follow me. LeRoy presented as a misogynist and he was obsessed with controlling me. When the line went down for tooling, the toolmaker came over and LeRoy backed away. When I restarted the line, LeRoy came up behind me quickly and sneered in my ear, "I'm still going to get 500 (parts)." Five hundred parts is the goal of built parts each area tries to achieve each day per shift. I had been keeping his line running. About a half hour later, the line went down again for tooling. He missed his parts.

When the toolmaker left, LeRoy stalked me the rest of his shift. I had the union steward write a grievance for me on January 30, 2003 against LeRoy. The next day he continued to follow me and tried to catch me in isolated areas.

I said to my union steward, "I am terrified of this man. He is always following me and trying to catch me alone. Do I have to file charges with the Pontiac police department or get a personal protection order?" My blood pressure was up and I was having trouble with my right eye. I had to visit the plant medical department for a short relief. After I wrote LeRoy up for harassment, his supervisor came over and told him, "Leave her alone." He was angry, but he did leave me alone, for a while until Amos Horace became his boss. This man was so volatile that I would cross the aisle to avoid passing him. I had tried to get away from him in an earlier incident and the supervisor's ,Camille, arm had shot out blocking my exit. She blocked my attempt to get away from a violent Leroy. She hit my wrist hard, hurting it, but there was nothing I could do although she had just assaulted me.

After the grievances were written, Jack Tolbin wanted to discuss them with me. I told Jack, "You know I can't speak with you without my union steward." Jack left in a huff and Amos Horace came to see me posing as a friend. I knew not to trust Amos. I told him that LeRoy only bothered the minority women and left the men alone. Amos stated, "It's probably due to his Mississippi upbringing." Amos was pretending to be my friend while trying to get my supervisor to write me up because I had written up LeRoy. I also had not ventured out of the plant to file charges against Jack, as Amos had tried to coerce me to do. I should have immediately gone to a government agency who protects workers from various discrimination. I was trying to correct the situation in-house.

Amos was the general foreman on the afternoon shift, and I was on the day shift. Amos bragged about being a deacon in his church. When I returned from my bereavement leave after a week because my biological father had passed. Amos began pressuring me to file charges against Jack. People become very interesting when they think you are stupid.

After I had to deal with all these wild men, Derek came to see me.

"Hey, what's up?" he asked.

"Nothing. I just got through dealing with LeRoy."

"He was bothering you again?"

"He's always after me."

"Well, come on, Camille, if there was no George, you wouldn't give me some?"

This is the type of ignorance I had to put up with.

"What's wrong with you? There is a George. The only thing we have in common is we're both Black and both electricians. You do not interest me. We're merely co-workers. I will NEVER sleep with you and you need to respect the fact that I'm married. Our worlds are 180 degrees apart. Leave me alone!" But it was all about what Derek wanted, and he wanted me, just to brag that he had me.

I walked away disgusted. No matter how many times I said no, I couldn't override that fantasy in his head of us sleeping together and him controlling me. He was a runt, scared of the other men. His fantasy world began to control every action he took with me. Derek could not speak two sentences without using the words "fuck" or "motherfucker." He described us Black women as "Bitches and Ho's." He did not know how to properly hold his eating utensils, gripping his fork in his fist as he shoveled food into his mouth. He allowed his 16 year old daughter's boyfriend to move in the house and sleep in the bed with her. He thought he was the smartest guy in the world because he knew the robots. He had worked with them for 12 years. I had never worked with robots before Pontiac. I found Derek, low educated, no class, disrespectful of Black women, a misogynist, a narcissist, a man who thought that every woman wanted that filth between his legs.

A few days later Derek was in another drug-induced state. He approached me and said something concerning the other Camille.

I said, "She needs to watch her nasty mouth. People think it's me."

He retorted, "You need to do something about your hair." I had nice braids that he didn't like.

I snapped back," You need to do something about your teeth." His teeth were in poor shape and needed a good cleaning.

"Why did you have to go there?" he cried.

"What? You think I'm going to let you talk about me and not say anything back?" I asked, amazed by his arrogance.

"That's what I do," he stated, with arrogance.

"Well, you may do it to these other women, and they allow you to; but you will not do it to me."

At that point his tone changed.

"You better not ever meet my girlfriend."

"Why?" I asked

"She's going to think you're the other Camille and she's going to whoop your ass."

"What do you think I'm going to be doing if your stupid girlfriend attacks me?"

He was chuckling at the thought of me being bloodied by his girlfriend.

"I guarantee, if your girlfriend attacks me I'm going to defend myself, including killing her if it comes to that. You would let your girlfriend attack me knowing it's not me sleeping with you and never will? You're sick."

I walked away with a clearer understanding of his lust for me. I could not turn to my union or management about Derek. If I reported the sexual harassment, all the tradesmen would turn against me and might cause me bodily harm, and there were hundreds of tradesmen. As far as GM was concerned, their supervisors thought it was funny. One had already thrown a condom in my work station area. I was alone. I didn't clearly understand everything about Derek's pursuit of me. He had told me he liked his women ghetto, not very bright, and not that attractive. They slept with him quicker. I was not ghetto, I was fairly attractive, I possessed brains, and I would never sleep with him. I felt sorrow for these women who gave their bodies freely to him while he had so little respect for them.

On March 18, 2003, I was working overtime to support production. I was sent to C-Zone to work with the regular electrician, Ben. His partner was off for the day. Reed Small said he wanted me to do preventive maintenance on the line.

I said, "The area has incoming and outgoing conveyors, and a transfer machine controlled by interlocking stations. Because of the nature of the line I need to pull the power disconnect on that particular cell."

He did not ask his regular man to perform the work. I did not mind doing the work, but wanted to do it safely.

Reed said, "I don't think you need to do that."

"Reed, I have spoken with the safety rep who assured me I was within my rights to do so. I have to wedge my body in the transfer machine to do the job and contend with the robots. The Monitored Power System does not constitute full Lock-Out under MiOSHA (Michigan Occupational Safety and Health Administration) standards. It is electrically controlled. Look it up on the Internet."

"I will personally help you lock out."

I asked in amazement, "You are telling me you will take personal responsibility for my safety?"

"Yes, I will."

"Reed, that is against General Motors lock-out policy. You can't assist me in locking out. GM does not want the liability."

"I'm going to get Amos."

I was speaking to the union steward, who happened to be Chad. This union official had no intentions of helping me. As Chad and I were speaking, Amos charged in, enraged.

Amos said, "If you pull that disconnect, I will use discipline and put you in the streets. There is nothing in there to injure you." Chad looked scared and ran away.

I recited what happened on L-Zone and asked, "Amos I need a hand written Safe Operating Procedure if you do not allow me to lock out. Can you guarantee nothing will move on me as it has before?"

Amos pressed his face close to mine, gritted his teeth and said, "I can't promise you you're going to live the next few minutes. Do the job or I will put you in the streets." I feared Amos would attack me. His eyes glazed over as he stared into mine, and I did the job unsafely, which is how factory workers are killed on the job. I feared Amos would attack me. No one would think my supervisor had threatened my life if I followed proper lock out procedures.

The following morning general foreman, Dylan Lukumski, wanted to talk to me about Amos. He said he promised Amos that he would straighten out the situation. Dylan knew that the lock-out issue was against GM policy and that I could have lost my life. Dylan Lukumski was a huge man. He stood at least 6"3" and weighed at least 350lbs. He had me closed in a small office while he tried to persuade me not to do anything about the lock out situation. His massive frame blocked the door and I could not get out of the office. His radio sounded and he was called away to a job. I had placed a call to my safety rep, and Lukumski was out of line. It was clearly another intimidation method.

I continued to seek help about the lock-out situation. My local union failed me and my International Union failed to address the matter. I wrote them three letters, and the union still did nothing. I was now lost as to whether or not I could lock-out the equipment myself or only when management gave me permission. If a supervisor wants a worker to perform a safety procedure their way, they are required to give the employee a hand written Safe Operating Procedure. Amos had refused my request for a Safe Operating Procedure when I requested one, which is also against GM policy. I avoided Amos as much as I could after that, but he was not going to allow me to avoid him too much. Again, Amos did not take kindly to any one challenging his words, and I knew it was a matter of time before he would be after me again. Amos reported to the day shift as general foreman.

This local management was intent on harassing good workers while allowing the White males with social issues to escalate their issues on GM property. There was a White male, Donnie Westgate, who decided he was going to "piss on the company." He was angry his TV was seized. He kept a TV in a locked cabinet in his area. He never wanted to work and when asked to do something extra, he would get angry. He took the term "pissing on the company" to a higher level. He began urinating on the machinery. The body shop was in an uproar. He would travel from line to line and urinate on the equipment, weld curtains and anything that was in his path. I walked in one morning and smelled the stench of urine. The weld curtains were dripping and pools of urine were on the floor. Disgusted I engaged in conversation with supervisor Phil Rocha about the situation.

"Phil, this is disgusting. You guys know who's doing this. You guys have to do something."

"We have to catch him in the act," he responded.

"You need to send him to a psychiatrist."

"We can't unless we catch him."

Not believing his indifference I said, "These are his body fluids. We shouldn't have to work around his disgusting body fluids. This is now a safety issue, you must take action."

"There's nothing we can do," and walked away.

Donnie soon tired of his games in the body shop and transferred to the paint department. He began the same sick activity there. One day, while having his fun, two supervisors walked past and he failed to see them. He sprayed them. They gave him 30 days off and he bumped back to the body shop to continue, "pissing on the company." He knew he could get by with the behavior there, and he did.

In July, 2003 Amos took me off the Infrared job and returned me to the line with Corky and LeRoy Brown. LeRoy had acquired Irvin Casey as his supervisor and Irvin did not prevent him from stalking me. Leon Stroh was my supervisor and I repeatedly requested him to order LeRoy to leave me alone.

I told Leon, "I am terrified of LeRoy and being in this isolated area with him."

Leon said, "LeRoy is a member of management, you have to answer to him regardless of your Dual Supervision. We don't give a crap." Dual supervision means that a worker reports to one supervisor under the Local agreement. Each plant negotiated an agreement specific to their plant. A local agreement never can supersede the National Agreement.

"I'm telling you I am afraid of him. He is volatile."

"He's a member of management. Deal with it."

On August 18, 2003 LeRoy followed me all day, and every time the line faulted he would charge at me screaming, "Camille, it's down again," even if it was on my partner's side. My MS began flaring. My right eye was giving me a lot of trouble and my legs were starting to drag.

A White male bumped to the first shift. He had six years with the company and his brother was the assistant plant manager. Kent Scott was sent to work on S-Right doors. Sam Zone, made the doors for the trucks and it had the Mig welder. It was not an easy area to run. When Kent bumped to this job assignment, he was not happy. He refused to do the job correctly. He took his time and constantly drained the bank of completed doors. LeRoy stayed away from him. Management decided that instead of making him do the job, they would switch him with me. I worked the area he had previously worked and he wanted it back. I was forced to work a much more difficult job. I had been on my job for over two years and because Kent refused to do his job, I was punished for it. I had 25 yrs seniority and Kent had 6..

I believe Amos Horace intentionally moved me to the area where my nightmare had begun. I began to have flashbacks of the terror I experienced in that zone. This was the same area where Stan stalked me and instilled fear in me.

I asked Hyman , "Whose decision is this to move me?"

He gave me four different answers. 1) I did not get along with Corky. Corky screamed at me and management blamed me. 2) They needed someone to help Corky repair the carriers. They had constantly tried to make me repair carriers that I had received no training in repairing. Corky and the other guys had received training 3) They were going to move Ramon but he got easily confused, 4) I'm the floater and this was a temporary move. Hyman, my current supervisor, wasn't very bright. None of it was true.

CHAPTER 11

I began my new job on August 19, 2003, the day after I wrote up LeRoy. This was going to become my permanent position. I asked Hyman, "Why are you switching me with Kent and holding me to a higher standard of work?" They expected me to perform work at a greater degree than any man. Hyman was silent and I asked for my union steward. Leslie, my union rep stated that management refused to return me to my former position and that I could forget about going back. The stress that management was putting on me was unrelenting. The numbness in my lower extremities began to spread throughout my body. I began to believe I was going to have to quit my job in order to survive my Multiple Sclerosis. I felt they were going to force me to choose between quitting or exacerbating my disease. GM managers didn't seem care how it was done. Then things became worse.

Saturday August 23, 2003 the weld monitor came over and told me he was getting porosity (dirt) on one weld. Weld monitors inspect the welds for quality. I asked him which torch. He said he did not know, although it was his and the operator's job to know. The torches are numbered and it could not get simpler than that. Charles was a very nervous man, and he had been given time off for allowing bad welds to get through the system. I entered the MIG welder and cleaned everything out. I restarted the line and watched a few doors go through the system without a problem. I returned to my main line. The production group leader approached me and said that Charles had told him that the welds were still bad. I told the group leader that I had done all that I knew how to do, and to please call my supervisor since I did not have a radio, and to please call the welding supervisor. My friend, Maurice Green, who was a Third Vice President of the North Oakland NAACP at the time, was there when this exchange took place and heard what I said.

My supervisor, Hyman, arrived and I accompanied him to the MIG. The weld supervisor, Matt, was also there. I explained to the weld supervisor that his weld monitor could not help me identify the torch that required intense, time-consuming maintenance, and I needed permission to keep the line down.

I told the weld supervisor, "I am not going to babysit a grown man. Make these people accountable for their own jobs. It is Charles' responsibility to know which torch the weld came from. He is supposed to know all the welds and their corresponding numbers. He's the weld expert for goodness sake." I had no training in inspecting welds. For this task I was totally unqualified.

Matt and Hyman entered the MIG welder. While they were there, Amos Horace came over and demanded to know why the line was down. I explained that Matt and Hyman were making a decision. They decided they wanted me to change tips and diffusers on torches 1 and 2. I did as instructed.

When I finished Hyman came over and said, "You changed the wrong torches."

"Hyman, you told me torches 1 and 2."

"That's not 1 and 2."

I replied, "It most certainly is."

Hyman went back into the cell and advanced the wire feed. He then realized he had instructed me to change the wrong torches. They never asked my opinion, had counted from right to left and the torches were numbered left to right. Instead of allowing me to do my job, which I knew well, they wanted to tell me how to do it while knowing hardly anything about the equipment.

Amos Horace was standing nearby and getting angry. Hyman was petrified with fear as he explained to Amos that he'd instructed me to change the wrong torches. Amos was livid and told Hyman to have me change the other two. Hyman (who had never given me any instructions on how he wanted me to maintain the MIG welder) decided he was going to put me on notice for "not helping to solve the weld quality problem," which was not a shop rule. A day after writing LeRoy up, I was now on "Notice of Reprimand." It is the responsibility of electricians who work in the weld lab to solve weld quality issues. They have the training. I returned to my line, and LeRoy walked around laughing at me.

I could not believe I was receiving all this harassment while I was actually following GM's shop rules. I was "not a team player," according to the electricians who were defrauding the company and the management who were allowing it, and even seemed to encourage it. I felt that management wanted me gone, and would go to any lengths to bring it about. I believed they were going to fire me, make me quit, or cause an exacerbation of my MS to the point where I would have no choice but to leave. There was nowhere for me to turn inside GM's infrastructure or within the union. The "open door" policy did not seem to work, and the complaining employee inevitably became the targeted employee. The *open door* policy means that one airs their grievances to higher management and face no retaliation for doing so. My body felt ready to explode into a serious exacerbation of my MS, and I was frightened. I knew my eyesight and mobility were at risk. So did this management.

On Sunday, August 24, 2003, Hyman instructed me to change wire spools, tips, nozzles, cups, liners, and diffusers on the MIG welder. On Monday, August 25, 2003, management brought in an electrician early to cover the other door line instead of getting Kent off a now one-man line. They refused to make him work. The next day when I arrived at work, the little sub-assembly I maintained was down. The sub-assembly was just a small machine that ran independent of the line. The midnight electrician was long gone and had left it down. The operator said someone had come over and cut off his maintenance call button and simply walked away. He placed the call again.

While servicing this equipment the operator informed me that the second shift had been sent home because the MIG welder was malfunctioning again. An outside welding company was called in to correct the ongoing problem, for which the management was now holding me solely responsible. I spoke with the welding company's agent who told me the welder had a bad motor and a faulty cord. The gun was making enough contact to weld, but not enough to produce good welds. On August 27, 2003, the MIG was down again when I arrived at work. The midnight electrician could not fix it and had also walked away from it. The problem indeed was a defective motor, which I simply changed.

Hyman told me the body shop had defective wire in the system and removed it because it was producing poor weld quality. All this time I was still on notice for the poor weld quality and wrongful allegations against me. Management did not hold the midnight or afternoon White male electricians, who had been on the job for years, who had been on the job 20 years longer to the same standard they held me. Jack Tolbin had come out to the welder knowing that the situation was not my fault, but he used Amos Horace, the Scripture-quoting Christian, to keep me *on* notice and continue the harassment. It is my opinion that this management figured this would not constitute discrimination because we were both Black. However, Jack Tolbin was still in charge of Amos Horace.

On August 28, 2003 my union steward, Leslie, came to see me. I asked him, "Why am I still on notice for something I have no control over and Jack Tolbin is aware of it?" Jack Tolbin was over all the supervisors and he told them what to do. Amos was the General Foreman at that time and Jack told him how to handle me. A lower ranking supervisor had to ask Jack Tolbin to do anything and Amos was a lower ranking supervisor. Leslie answered, "Amos refuses to move you back to your line but he will move you to a different line." Leslie refused to answer my question. Jack Tolbin always had the lower management do his business and Amos was the chosen bully this time. Amos enjoyed this because it was another way of controlling me and Amos was a control freak with women.

I replied, "I will not displace another electrician and get him angry with me. I don't need any more hostility towards me."

Leslie said he agreed to keep me on notice. He kept telling me that Amos wanted an interview with Labor Relations and me. I told him OK. He thought I did not understand and repeated this to me. I told him to set the interview up because all I wanted was a piece of paper with their names on it. Leslie stormed off stating that the interview would be set up. As he walked away, I crossed the aisle to see where he was going. Leslie did not see me, but I saw plenty.

Amos Horace was around the corner with his arms folded, a smug look on his face and his leg on the guardrail as he waited for Leslie. Then I watched them converse for a minute and saw Amos's face registering outrage. He did not seem to like what Leslie was telling him. I circled around them as I headed to my welder. They were engrossed in conversation as they walked hurriedly towards my main line and they didn't see me. A fault came up on the marquee that the Mig welder wasn't running. I didn't get my safety lock on the gate to the welder before Amos appeared and took me off notice.

He said, "Camille, I'm taking you off notice, but we will still have a conversation in Labor Relations." Employees were often frightened to deal with GM Labor Relations. I just looked at him. I had not violated any shop rules. Amos decided to intimidate me with going to Labor Relations.. Labor Relations had the power to fire employees

On August 29, 2003, the weld monitor came over and told me that porosity was accumulating on torch #3. I walked over to clean the welder. The weld lab employees were there, along with Matt, their supervisor. When I was done, I returned to my main line. 20 minutes later I was summoned back to the welder. The weld monitor had turned the conveyor to manual mode and failed to return it to auto mode when he walked away. This would drain the bank of truck doors. In manual mode the conveyor does not run and finished doors do not move through the system. I spoke to his supervisor and asked him to instruct his people to return the conveyor to automatic mode. There would not be a signal fault or alarm to alert anyone that the conveyor was not running.

At 7:57 AM the weld monitor loaded the door at the weld check conveyor improperly and the robot crashed into it. The door was hanging tightly on the robot, and I needed assistance to remove it. I called for the millwrights. They were on another job and not available to assist me (even though we had several pairs of millwrights). They were full size truck doors weighing 52 lbs and awkward in shape. I needed the door lifted off the robot so that I would not damage the robot and cause excessive down time. The millwrights finally came and carefully removed the door. My right eye was giving me problems and I called for my supervisor to obtain a pass to medical. I had previously gone almost blind in my right eye from optic neuritis, and it seemed this was happening again. Supervisor, Percy Skeeter, responded to my call.

I said, "Percy, I'm sick. My MS is flaring and I need a pass to *medical.*"

Percy said, "Stay here and I'll bring you one." I waited for him, but he did not return.

Twenty minutes later Hyman pulled up on a vehicle. "Do you have my pass to medical?" I asked

"No!"

"I asked Percy for a pass 20 minutes ago, and he hasn't returned with it."

"Are you okay?"

"No, my MS is flaring and I need to go to medical immediately!"

"Hop on the cart and we'll go to the office and get your pass."

I hopped on the cart with Hyman and we headed to the maintenance office. At first, I did not realize what was going on. I was feeling very ill and my eye was giving me problems. Hyman went into the office. I glanced in and saw Jack Tolbin, Amos Horace from the management team, and Stuart Ralston and Leslie Beckman for the union. Apparently, the meeting was being set up for today and I had no idea. Hyman came out of the office and I again asked for my pass.

Hyman said, "You are not going anywhere until we have this meeting."

I replied weakly, "My MS is flaring and I need a pass to *medical.*"

"You walk in the office and get it."

"Hyman my legs are not working properly and you are my supervisor. You can't refuse me a pass to medical."

"We are having a meeting with you right now."

"Hyman, are you refusing me a pass to medical?"

He hunched over me, flexed his muscles and said, "Yes, I guess I am."

I think I went into shock. I had never in all my years with GM, been refused a pass to medical. As I sat on the cart, I saw the area manager, Terry Vendenberg in his office. I managed to walk weakly into Terry's office to inform him that Hyman had denied me a pass to medical. I needed Terry to order him to grant my pass. Management cannot refuse an employee medical treatment, but this management did. Terry ordered Amos to give me a pass. Amos Horace said, "You can leave but we will still have that talk in Labor." He issued my pass.

I knew Amos was upset because I tried to get some help concerning the lock-out situation and I had not filed charges against Jack. I knew it was just a matter of time before he came after me again and he was coming out full force. Jack Tolbin knew I was not responsible, but he was angry about the class action lawsuit. He knew there was nothing I could do. He should have stopped Amos, since he was Amos's supervisor. Jack would have been surprised to learn that Amos was tutoring me on how to file charges against him.

Amos had previously told me that in his religious belief, the man was the boss and the woman followed his rules. He would become upset when I did not want to listen to his religious proselytizing. Amos continued to come after me because I was Black, female and a I was a vunerable target for him. He knew he could do just about anything to me and Labor Relations would not assist me because we were both Black, and thus, it would most likely would not constitute discrimination. He was terrified of the Queen, a White woman. I therefore decided to head to the Michigan Department of Civil Rights instead and filed gender discrimination charges against Amos on September 3, 2003. He was making more demands on my weakened body and I knew he would come after me again. My union had stalled me and my time to file a charge was running out.

My union steward, Leslie, smirked, "You have to resolve all internal solutions before you can go outside and file charges." This union did nothing for me. It was just six years of wasted union dues.

On September 5, 2003, I was summoned to Labor Relations. Although the Skilled Trades Labor rep was a White male, there was a substitute in his place. Amos sought out the new Black production Labor rep, Ronnie Moore, to conduct the interrogation. I did not know how familiar Ronnie was with skilled trade issues, but using a Black man to continue to harass me was the nature of the beast. In this meeting, there were three people from management: general foreman Amos Horace, supervisor Hyman Stolz, and Labor rep, Ronnie Moore. For the union there was Zone man, Stuart Ralston, alternate union steward Bing Landwehr, and me. Stuart, it seemed, was setting me up with management. I had brought attention to the co-workers (his friends) who were stoned on the job and defrauding the company, and he was not happy with me.

As Amos was speaking, I pulled a notebook and pen from my purse and began to write. He became nervous, his eyes widened, and he sucked in his breath. He had begun this process. It seemed he no longer wanted to proceed, with me writing everything down, but it was too late for him to turn back without losing face.

Amos began to spin his version why I was placed *on notice*.

I asked, "Amos, how do you know why I was placed on notice? You were not there and I am not on notice. This is simply a little chat in front of Labor."

Hyman then mumbled that he had placed me on notice for failure to help solve the weld quality problem. Again, Amos resumed his tale of why they had put me on notice. Management was aware that there was nothing I could do about the weld quality problem. The specially trained electricians in the weld lab were trained to solve the problem.

"Hyman , where did you get this information?"

Hyman said proudly, "From the production group leader." Amos tried to shush Hyman to keep him from admitting he had placed me on notice on hearsay, but it was too late.

Amos told me, "You are going to answer to anyone who says anything to you. Weld monitors, operators, production workers or their group leaders. If you do not, I will issue you a discipline."

Other hourly workers did not have the authority or skills to order me around. Ronnie Moore was unaware that we had a dual supervision agreement with management. According to this agreement, I reported to one supervisor except in cases of emergency. I produced the agreement. My other plants all had dual supervision rules and they ran efficiently. It cut out all the chaos. Management had also signed the agreement and agreed to abide by it.

Amos stated that he moved me because management had the right to make job assignments, and because I did not get along with Corky. Management does have the right to job assignment, but they're to be issued fairly, in an Equal Opportunity environment, to root out discrimination. I informed Ronnie that Corky screamed and yelled at me, and told him that management needed to send him to anger management classes. Instead, they tried to punish me. Amos then stated, and Hyman concurred, that neither of them had ever heard Corky yell at anyone. When I looked at Amos's face, I felt I was looking into the eyes of true evil. Christian? My behind.

I said, "Amos, there you go lying again."

My Zone man, Stuart, finally spoke up. He told Labor, "I have spoken with this guy on several occasions and he *is* pretty excitable. She does not have to accept that type of behavior from him. I have to deal with it as part of my job."

I informed Labor, "I asked the union to step in and speak to management about Corky's attitude nine months ago. Apparently, management left me in a 'hostile work environment' for that period of time."

At this point, Amos Horace nervously backed up, stumbling over his words, saying, "I know nothing about this since I was not on the shift then."

I said, "So why are you bringing it up now?" Hyman sat back looking like a dull knife. He didn't have a clue of what was happening.

Amos smirked, "I can transfer you out of the body shop."

I said, "No thanks. You will make a call, and the harassment would get worse. You will then try to prove I could not get along with anyone while you place my life in greater danger."

Amos knew the defective cultural mentality of the plant was campus wide. I would not settle for anything less than a transfer off that campus. I would have transferred in a minute, but the rules of transfer did not allow me to do so. Another plant would have to request an electrician, and then the plant where the employee was currently working had to agree to let you go. It was also based on seniority, and many electricians wanted to leave Pontiac Truck.

Amos mentioned the day the robot crashed and I could not move the door. The weld monitor had caused the crash by improperly loading the door on the conveyor. There was no way I could have lifted that fifty-two pound door by myself. It was the weld monitor who had caused the excessive down time and it took two strong, male millwrights to remove the door. One had to climb on top of the conveyor to remove it without causing more damage to the robot.

Amos said, "I will not move you back to your line, but I will send you to another line." Amos decided that he would send me to U-Zone Left. He told Labor Relations the doors were smaller and that this would remove me from LeRoy's area. The doors were 38 lbs and still too heavy and awkward for me to manage on my own; but there was another reason for this move.

U-Zone left was manned by my harasser, Stan Minard. Management knew that he would be upset with the replacement and the harassment would become harsher. I certainly could not count on this management to intervene, and Amos knew that. He brought up the incident concerning a door that had crashed on the lifter. I had been on the other end taking care of another problem when this occurred. The two electricians from Control Support were standing there when the crash occurred, and no one moved. They should have taken care of the problem themselves. They were electricians. When I finished the job I was on, I proceeded to the new crash. Everyone was looking and otherwise doing nothing, including Amos and Hyman. When I entered the cell. The door was stuck and refused to budge. I asked for Hyman 's assistance, and he had a difficult time with the door as well.

Hyman then ordered me to raise the lifter, not realizing that the robot was in position to remove the door and that I would crash the lifter into the robot, damaging the equipment. They would have then issued a discipline to me for following the supervisor's order. There was a motor driving the conveyor that was a lot stronger than I was, and the door would not budge.

I said to Hyman in the Labor office, "Hyman, you could not budge the door yourself. Look at you and look at me. You are a weight lifter. How do you expect me to move it and you couldn't?"

Stuart Ralston spoke up finally and told Amos, "You then would have tried to discipline her for that."

Amos said, "No, we allow for human error."

It made no sense. I was sitting in the Labor office for situations I had no control over, and he was saying he allows for human error. Again, the men who had been on this job for years could not fix the problem, but I was the one sitting in the Labor office within two weeks of being returned to the place where my nightmare began.

I finally asked Ronnie, "If I can't move the door, what am I supposed to do?"

Ronnie answered, "Call the millwrights."

I replied, "That's what I did. Amos is trying to railroad me and set me up."

It was a final decision by Amos to move me to U-Zone to smaller but still heavy and awkward doors. He stated that it would also remove me from LeRoy Brown's presence.

On Saturday, September 6, 2003, I encountered defective material that did not make the switch proximity which caused a fault. The proximity switch indicates that the material is in position for the needed operation. LeRoy would see the faults on the monitor in his office and follow me to all the jobs. Supervisors normally have more to do than follow the electrician around but LeRoy enjoyed harassing me. At 10:10 AM, an improperly loaded door by the production workers had welded to the machine.

Although the welder was not loaded properly the machine still welded the door to the machine. Amos walked over and spoke to LeRoy. LeRoy's face looked gleeful and his interest in me grew more intense. I got the line back running.

During my partner's lunch break, I had to watch his line and MIG also. There was a crash on his line and that the door was stuck to the machine. I called for the millwrights. They needed to pry the door loose with a pry bar. I was working by myself with two lines, two MIG welders, four conveyors, and a sub-station to maintain. I heard my line go down, but I was currently on another job.

LeRoy flew over in a frenzy. He screamed at me, "You need millwrights! Have you called the millwrights?" all the while charging towards me with rage burning in his eyes. I escaped behind a large basket to separate us. LeRoy, attempted to maneuver himself around the basket, still yelling, "Have you called the millwrights, Camille? Have you called the millwrights?" while advancing towards me. Again I moved out of his reach. His face was twisted and his fists clenched. He looked as if he could strangle me at any time. He was trying to force me to interact with him regardless of the fear I had of him. I clenched the awl in my apron tightly. If he had come within six inches of me, I would have put the awl through him. The millwrights arrived, and I believe they prevented him from assaulting me. LeRoy backed quickly away and left the scene.

From September 8-16, 2003, I worked the Infrared job while Prince was on vacation. I had asked Amos for the next available vacation day, which he said would be September 17th. I wanted to amend my complaint to include retaliation for the ongoing lawsuit which I was a part of. Four of us worked in the body shop. I had been overwhelmed by the abuse when I filed my original complaint, fighting off a major exacerbation of my MS, and did not get everything on paper.

GM had changed directions and was now using the Black males to come after me. A man who had less seniority time also requested September 17th as a vacation day and was granted priority over me. When I mentioned this to Amos, he said he remembered my requesting it. But then he tried to blame the supervisor, telling me he was "not saying that Hyman did not backdate Damon's application."

On September 18, I reported to my new job at 6:30 AM. The first supervisor I saw that morning was LeRoy Brown. All morning he paraded himself around my area, making sure I saw him. Amos had told the Labor rep he was moving me away from LeRoy. Yet now LeRoy was now working in my new area. I began to accumulate defense weapons from my toolbox in case he backed me into a corner.

A few days later, as I was taking my lunch break in the millwright area, I saw Jack Tolbin rushing toward the front office with Amos Horace in tow. Jack made eye contact with me when he returned. The look on his face told me my charges had hit. He kept staring at me in amazement. Amos did not speak to me, but he frequented my area letting me know he was present and could come around me as he pleased. Jack was gone for the next couple of weeks. Things ran better without him stirring up confusion.

CHAPTER 12

My health was deteriorating as my body reacted to the constant stress. I was having problems with my eyes, my legs were dragging, and my balance was off. I was experiencing slight incontinence, cold feet and more numbness in the arms. On October 1, 2003 I saw my neurologist, Dr. William Leuchter, and explained what was going on at work. He gave me a referral to a psychologist, Dr. Louis Dvorkin. I knew I was in trouble. It took a couple of days, but I finally got the courage to call him and make an appointment for October 9, 2003. I had been avoiding seeing a psychologist because of the stigma attached to it, but my body was reacting to the relentless stress I was undergoing, with no relief in sight. I knew I needed his help.

We received a new area manager and Jack Tolbin returned from his hiatus. I ventured over to my assigned MIG welder to clean it out and realized that the conveyor had stopped moving doors through the MIG station. A fault did not register, and so an alarm did not sound to alert me. I stopped Jack to inform him of this situation as it could have a negative impact on our through-put. Through-put is the smooth flow of truck parts through our system.

Stan began to appear in my area again. He was upset with me for taking his job, and I once again began to fear for my safety. This job assignment was Amos's idea. This was the pitiful, stereotypical image this management held of Black males and the way they abuse Black females. Amos sent me to take Stan's job because he knew Stan would be angry with me and harass me further. Amos was really angry that he could not control me with religion. I never understood why all these men were trying to control me. Man after man was trying to force me to do things their way. These managers were willing to abuse a Black female for their own purposes of getting promotions with the company. I was in the lawsuit against GM and they were retaliating. This management seemed to view Blacks as the scum of the earth, and Amos, Leroy, and Derek were doing a great job enhancing this idea.

When I visited Dr. Dvorkin, I told him my painful story. I knew he was worried because he spent two hours with me. He immediately suggested that I take at least a 30-day leave of absence. I had programmed myself to report to work every day regardless of how I felt, and had not missed a day of work in over two years despite my debilitating disease. He asked if I could come back next week, and at least ponder his suggestion in the meantime.

The following week I reported four hours early to support production. I had agreed to cover another electrician who wanted time off. The stress was escalating and the MS was continuing to give me problems. During my second visit, Dr. Dvorkin again spent two hours with me. He asked me if I had thought over his suggestion. Considering the way I was feeling, I concurred with his opinion.

I had agreed to work the weekend, but had one day to change my mind. (This was another new rule.) I told Dr. Dvorkin I would cancel my weekend, but on the day I cancelled my supervisor, Dillion, approached me saying that he had bad news for me. He explained that the body shop needed a certain number of people for the weekend. Since I had low overtime hours I would be forced to work when I didn't want to.

When the job assignments came out I was not needed in the Body Shop, I was banished to the paint department. The job would more than likely be more strenuous. The job assignment the previous weekend required me to hang 130 lb, eight-foot light fixtures with three men on ladders and no hoist to hold the fixture, which was hard on my back and arms. Also, my balance was off because of the MS, so I had to be especially careful. GM's ladder safety required three-point contact at all times on a ladder. Two feet and one arm, or two arms and one foot must maintain contact. I used both arms to hold the fixture, but had to stretch out at an angle that caused my foot to leave the ladder and not maintaining three point contact. I could have fallen off the ladder and injured myself. It is impossible to maintain three point contact on jobs, you need both hands to do the work but this management seemed intent on harming me.

On Friday, October 17, 2003, I tried one last time to get some assistance from the union with my decision not to work the weekend. I should not be forced to work. The management was amused with my predicament. Leroy Brown peeped his head into my area, smirking at me. When I saw him, I grabbed a 12 inch screwdriver, prepared to plunge it into his heart if necessary. When I headed to the ladies' restroom the next day, I saw Stan Minard circling my line.

The ladies' room was a windowless brick building sitting isolated in the Body Shop. Lights are always supposed to be on in the bathrooms, along with exit signs. When I opened the door slightly, I saw that it was pitch black inside. I started to reach in and feel for the light switch, and then I pulled my hand back in fear. The emergency exit sign was also black. Someone had cut the power to it. I was the only female working maintenance that weekend. With threats being made against my life, I didn't know if a man might be on the other side of the door waiting to grab me. I was a prime target and no one would hear anything once I was inside. I retreated in fear. That was the first time I'd experienced finding the lights off in that bathroom. I didn't want to become the guest of honor at a "blanket party." The guests at these *parties* are quickly snatched, blankets are tossed over them, and they are beaten. I know a man who was "guest" at a blanket party inside GM. The bathroom is soundproof, so no one would hear anything once you're inside. Assailants aren't identified because the blanket covers your eyes.

Since these were Derek's friends, I didn't know how far they would go. They knew he was trying to sleep with me and that I wasn't responding. If they got me into the pitch-black bathroom they could assault me. I felt that Derek would take sex by force since that was the only way he would get it or Necrophilia. Derek wanted to exert complete dominance over me. The plants don't share with the public the fact that sexual assaults are committed against female workers, but it's known around the work-force. There are many places to attack someone that go unnoticed. Plants are like little crime riddled cities. Women are treated as sex objects by many men. Derek was what I would call a "sex fiend." He was living and sleeping with his ex-wife's ex-best friend. He was a hound. He wanted me badly and didn't care that I was married. I didn't think he would assault me if he were sober, but he and his friends were always in drug induced states of mind and these drug addicts could do anything without being held accountable for their actions. These idiots mixed their drugs with alcohol.

I never told my husband what Derek, his crew, and GM management were doing to me. I didn't want him to react and then be in jail for things

GM and the UAW could have stopped. What man would sit quietly while other men are harassing his wife?

I'd had enough of the mental and physical punishment, supervisors all over me, Stan threatening to kill me, Derek sexually harassing me and trying to control me, and getting no help from GM or the UAW, so I headed to the medical department. When I rang the little doorbell to enter medical, a nurse came to the door and snapped, "I'm busy, what do you want?" When I explained that I had a note from Dr. Dvorkin to the plant medical doctor, she allowed me in. The doctor checked my blood pressure after I had rested an hour. Her eyes widened as she did a recheck. It was 158/90. I normally have low blood pressure; it had never been that high. The doctor immediately issued me a letter of disability to give to my supervisor because of the high blood pressure.

I returned to my area, put all my tools away, cleaned up everything that was mine, gave my supervisor my paperwork from the plant doctor, and left. I have never returned. In essence, I was forced to leave my employment even though I had abided by all the company rules. Unfortunately, I was the only one playing by the rulebook. Because of my experience in other plants, I had put false faith in the management and the UAW, and they both failed me. The damage done to me psychologically took years to repair. As an optimist, over the years at the Pontiac plant, I continued to believe things would change for the better. That was one of my biggest mistakes.

I had spent quite some time dealing with my union on the lock-out issue. When I finally filed formal charges against Amos, the filing time was running out. S. J. Bashen the human resources firm that GM hired wanted to do early resolution as they called it and try to settle the case out of court. I agreed as long as they dealt with my attorney, Richard T. Taylor. There was no way I would ever deal with them again, especially by myself. Amos had placed me in a position where I could have been killed, and no one cared. Attorney Taylor and I didn't settle because S.J Bashen didn't want to deal with my attorney.

January 5, 2004 was the day of my scheduled deposition meeting with the GM attorney. The first deposition was cancelled by my attorney Richard T. Taylor who was hired by attorney H. Wallace Parker to oversee the handling of the cases of the class action litigants originally filed by the law office. He told me he was a Civil Rights attorney and fully capable of handling my case.

S. J. Bashen called my house seven times to talk to me just before my deposition. They wanted to set up a meeting with me alone, bypassing the EEOC, to which gender harassment case had been transferred. The EEOC now had jurisdiction over the case. S. J. Bashen did not meet with me earlier but in the confusion surrounding the transferring of my case, they contacted me personally. I referred them to my attorney, Richard T. Taylor, and made it clear that I would never meet with them again without my attorney present. They were not happy and must have contacted the GM attorney immediately, as the attorney for GM asked me about it in my deposition.

During the deposition, The GM attorney asked me if I thought that the supervisors would back off me if I yelled, cursed, and acted out. I replied that this was not part of my character. He also entered a document into evidence as "defendant exhibit 1." It was an incorrect copy of the vacation schedule which violated our National Agreement, provided by the inept local management. It was not according to the agreement negotiated by our National union, but what the local management had tried to negotiate. A local agreement can never supersede the National agreement. I provided GM's attorney with the correct copy.

The gender harassment case was in the hands of the EEOC now. The GM attorney, Alex Alexopolous, from Hardy, Lewis & Page in Birmingham, MI had a great time questioning me on all matters dealing with the EEOC case since they are allowed to ask anything they want in depositions. During the deposition Alex asked me, "Did your husband tell you that he was going to divorce you?" "What?", I asked. He repeated the question. He spoke as if he had spoken directly to my husband and my husband had told him that. He was trying to shake me up. Attorney Richard Terrell Taylor was a no show to the scheduled deposition. I was without proper representation since the substitute who came to my deposition had no knowledge of my case. All during this time, I was having multiple problems with the MS. It felt as though I was on the verge of a major attack. My eyes were blurry, my legs were dragging, and my body felt as if was having a big allergic reaction. I think the one thing that saved me was my weekly injections of Avonex, which helped to decrease the frequency of relapse symptoms.

A month later, I received a "right-to-sue" letter from the EEOC. I never once spoke to the EEOC investigator. S.J. Bashen also does investigations for the EEOC but they were paid but General Motors for an earlier report that they refused to give me or the union. A letter stating GM's defense had been was provided to me earlier. The report stated that supervisor Reed Small personally offered to assist me in locking out. The supervisor (a General Motors agent) decided he would take personal responsibility for my safety. If I had been hurt, he assumed the responsibility. I did not realize the safety rules had changed. So, according to the information that I have in writing, one's safety is the responsibility of the company and not the worker.

Not one grievance was written on my behalf by my union representatives for the blatant safety violations. I find that deplorable. My union basically told me, "Shame on you for doing the job." They said I should have taken the discipline and allowed the UAW to "work on it" after their refusal to help me. Had I taken the discipline of the balance of the shift and two days off for disobeying a direct order, upon my return the crew would have nailed me for anything they could, constantly disciplining me until they could justify terminating me. The terminated employee is often reinstated on a "last chance agreement." The next infraction, real or not (and there is always a next infraction waiting for the employee), results in permanent termination, with no legal recourse. And the UAW allowed this.

When General Foreman Amos threatened me about locking out the equipment, he should have provided me with a handwritten "Safe Operating Procedure" according to GM standards. He did not. Chad, who was then the union steward, should have headed directly to Labor and reported the situation. He was happy to assist management because he's the one who started the harassment. I did not stand a chance. Chad then received a nice job as an appointee with the International Union. He was rewarded for his actions while I had to retire on disability. I had suffered discrimination based on race, gender and disability, safety violations, death threats, and extreme sexual harassment. Chad went on to get a cushy job with the Union; Stan Minard died of a drug overdose; Derek continued getting drunk and high, and bedding as many women as he could. Amos, Jack, and LeRoy continued on as supervisors. No one answered for their actions against me. The stress of GM and corrupt courts left me unable to walk.

CHAPTER 13

On March 16, 2004, my class action court case against GM went to mediation in an attempt to resolve the case before it went to court. There were three attorneys involved. One was supposed to represent GM, one to represent me, and the other to remain neutral. When I found the names of the attorneys in my file, I wondered which one represented me. They added insult to injury by downplaying what had been done to me. They offered me $4,500, which I rejected. If I accepted the $4,500, I would have to remain silent about my ordeal as part of the agreement. I refused that offer. It was never about the money. It was about justice for the numerous women who are harassed every day in the auto industry by men who have power over them. I did not receive any justice.

On May 24, 2004, I received a very interesting phone call at home. Camille, the Black female manager, she had access to my personal records and had found my phone number. She had a story to tell me. She was out on a medical stress leave. She told me she had purchased a gun because she wanted to shoot general foreman, Amos Horace. My leaving had limited his choice of females to harass, and she had become his new target. When she snapped under the pressure, she began seeing a psychiatrist. When she confided her plan to shoot Amos, he sent her to a hospital in Detroit, thus preventing the shooting. She told me that they were going to lock her up in the mental ward. Her boyfriend retrieved the gun and turned it in to remove the threat. Because her boyfriend turned the gun in the hospital felt the threat was over and she was not locked up. This incident illustrates how hostile the work environment actually was. Pontiac Truck was perched on a powder keg.

On June 16, 2004, my case was presented before an Oakland County Circuit Court Judge, John James McDonald. My attorney, Richard T. Taylor, told me I would not be allowed to attend, and refused to give me any more information than that. The Judge made summary disposition in favor of General Motors on all counts. He even dismissed the complaint the EEOC had investigated, for which it had granted me a right-to-sue. He decertified the class action initiated by attorney H. Wallace Parker and controlled all the remaining cases himself.

The litigants in the class action case had a meeting with H. Wallace Parker, who told us what the judge had done. He provided us with no legal documentation. H. Wallace Parker filed the original class action suit. He then abandoned the suit and hired attorney Richard Terrell Taylor to manage the 15 remaining cases.

Attorney Taylor did not give me anything in writing; it was all verbal. The superintendent, Jack Tolbin had previously stated that he had removed me from the coveted Controls Support job just because I had MS, which violated the ADA act, a Federal law. The "Americans with Disabilities" act prevents employers from making discriminating decisions based solely on disabilities. The employer must prove that I could not perform the job. The judge called my removal from the job an "isolated incident." GM had admitted this discrimination to my UAW Civil Right rep., Martin Ramirez.

At this point, my faith in our justice system was shattered. A judge's duty is to uphold the law with impartiality and fairness. I was naive and believed this. I abided by all the rules, and yet my complaints were systematically dismissed. Not one plaintiff in the class action prevailed. Everyone couldn't have been wrong.

I finally realized that the "law" is in the service of the powerful. Within the GM work environment, Blacks could be called "niggers" and a GM supervisors could use the term "nigger piling." There were KKK outfits, Confederate flags, swastikas and personal safety violations of MiOSHA standards that were also contrary to GM's own safety standards. It seemed that the judges just didn't care.

I had worked peacefully for many years as a good employee of General Motors, a company I once loved dearly. I know that not all GM plants operate like the one in Pontiac, but the effort managers expended harassing me should have gone into running the plant more efficiently. Obviously, they had plenty of time and not enough to do. Then again, I had never seen so much management congregated in one area either.

I called my attorney, Mr. Taylor, the day after the hearing wanting to know what had happened. He told me that the judge would take a couple of weeks to formulate his opinion; but it came sooner than expected. Two days after the hearing," *Judge*" McDonald's opinion was in Mr. Taylor's hands. My case had gone before Judge McDonald on June 16, 2004. It flew through the court and was adjudicated with lightning speed. The entire process from the hearing to the rendering of the judge's opinion, the typing of the decision by a clerk, and its time-stamping by the Register of Deeds to indicate that it was received by my attorney on June 18 2004. It took two days. Judge McDonald had dismissed all counts against GM through summary disposition, which forced me to file an appeal and pay the court sanctions that GM sought against me. Adding insult to injury, my last name was misspelled on the decision. I told Mr. Taylor to file an appeal as soon as he sent me the judge's opinion.

I saw Taylor at a restaurant on July 29, 2004. He promised me he was filing it. When I called his office later to check, he swore he had filed the appeal and he had not. Judge McDonald had stated in his written opinion that the only course of action I had was to apply for Workers' Compensation which he knew I had already filed. GM's attorney was aware that I had filed the Worker's Compensation claim because of the emotional and physical damage done to my mind and body from the stress of constant harassment. He drilled me about it while taking my deposition. The Workers Compensation case went on for ten years and was more corrupted than the seven billion dollar civil case that I was part of filed by H.Wallace Parker. GM changed attorneys numerous times and subjected me to return visits to their Independent Medical Exam (IME) doctors. They played the rules their way. Michigan law states that claimants can bring forth a lawsuit for an intentional tort and I had a right-to-sue letter from the EEOC. http://www.a2lawyer.com/articles/injury/personal.html According to Michigan law this defines what a plaintiff can bring a civil suit for

After reading the judge's written opinion, I went into shock. This was America, and GM had admitted to discriminating against me. I moped around in disbelief for about two weeks. The judge was forcing me to file an appeal. I had done everything the correct way, by the book, and was still being stifled by those in charge of "the system". It was the final slap in my face. Although the legal system seemed prepared to allow GM to disregard the laws of the United States, I was not. I had suffered horribly at the hands of my male co-workers and GM management at this particular plant. What GM allowed to happen to me, I and others consider criminal.

It was intentional and malicious. I pulled out the notes that I had taken over the years and began to write the first edition of this book.

I waited patiently for my appeal to come up. Numerous cases that were filed after mine had gone through the appellate court. I saw this on the Internet through my Internet access to the Michigan Court of appeals. I tried to contact my attorney, but he was not returning my calls or letters. I was soon to find out why. On March 16, 2006, I was able to meet with the original attorney on my case, H.Wallace Parker. He said he had found my file in attorney Richard Taylor's old desk. What I discovered later was more shocking. Taylor had never filed my appeal. I suspect now that a deal may have been struck, without my consent, between the two attorneys since I never paid the $3,000 in sanctions that GM had won in an unfair ruling against me.

I was finally able to see a copy of the transcript of my deposition in my legal file. Fully108 pages of my 271-page deposition, 40% of it, had been removed. All of the pertinent, negative testimony against GM was missing. The deposition had been "bleached", and it was clearly not an accident. Blocks of 16 and 20 pages were missing. How could I have received effective representation with 108 pages of my deposition missing? It was a copy of the GM attorney's deposition transcript. Not only were there pages missing, but pages were crossed off on the copy. Apparently, as he was working the GM attorney crossed off pages he didn't want to use in GM's defense. But how did my attorney, Richard Taylor, not realize that 108 pages were missing from my deposition transcript? Was he stupid, or was he colluding with the defense attorney? Richard Taylor waited 10 days after receiving the judge's decision to contact me about filing my appeal. He wasted 10 precious days, and then he still did not file my appeal. I bought my own copy of the deposition and I have the GM copy also so what did the law H. Wallace Parker's firm do with the $1000 I had given them?

Stuffed into my file I also found my original right-to-sue letter issued by the Equal Employment Opportunity Commission. Attorney Taylor, it seems, never filed it. Had I been allowed to observe the court proceedings, I would have realized something was wrong. I believe this is the reason Richard Taylor banned me from coming to the hearing in the first place. He possessed a copied version of my deposition with pages crossed out. It presented a distorted and misleading version of the facts. I have since obtained a complete copy of my deposition transcript, which I had to obtain at my own expense a second time, although I had paid the law firm $1,000. I paid another $900 to buy my own deposition in order to get the complete deposition.

As my case went before Judge McDonald, another, much more publicized case was also being heard in his courtroom. It was the case of a Farmington Hills school teacher, Nancy Seaman, who was accused of murdering her husband with an axe. The case was the subject of a book, Internal Combustion, by Joyce Maynard. Seaman claimed abuse as her defense, but the jury did not believe she had proven her claim. They found her guilty of first-degree murder that judge McDonald reversed.

I found it ironic that judge McDonald told Nancy Seaman that, if she had reached out for help, she might not be in the position she currently found herself, facing life in prison. He then overrode the jury's decision and reduced her sentence because he believed she should have been convicted of second-degree murder. The prosecution appealed his decision, and it was overturned, with the Court of Appeals finding that judge McDonald had "improperly inserted himself as a thirteenth juror."

McDonald saw abuse in her case, although the abuse was clearly not seen by the people on the jury who convicted her. In my case however, he completely ignored my evidence. I had witnesses, letters addressed to GM and my union begging for help, and United States Post Office return receipts proving they had received the letters. I've always wondered why he handled the two cases so differently. Was it because Nancy Seaman was a fair-haired, White woman, and I am a Black woman? She may have been abused, but the difference in the way McDonald handled each of our cases is alarming. I neither hurt nor killed anyone. Would he have said the same to me about reaching out for help if I had ended in front of him for defending my life? I did reach out for help, using every legal means provided to me as a GM worker.

How could McDonald do this? Even if only in the interest of appearing fair, at least one case against GM should have made it to trial inside his court. Nancy Seaman's case was big news locally. As much as anyone else, as much as Nancy Seaman, I deserved to be treated with respect, compassion, and according to law.

STATE OF MICHIGAN
IN THE CIRCUIT COURT FOR THE COUNTY OF OAKLAND

CAMILLE MCMILLEN,

                Plaintiff,

v

GENERAL MOTORS COPR.,

                Defendants.

Case No.   03-047-272-CZ
Hon.   JOHN J. McDONALD

_____/

OPINION AND ORDER

At a session of Court held
in the City of Pontiac, County of
Oakland, State of Michigan, on

June 16, 2004.

PRESENT: HON. JOHN J. McDONALD
                   CIRCUIT COURT JUDGE

This matter is before the Court upon Defendant's motion for summary disposition (apparently pursuant to MCR 2.116 (C)(7)(statute of limitations) (8)(failure to state a claim), and (10)(no genuine issue of material fact). Plaintiff has alleged discrimination against Defendant based upon her sex and African American race as well as claims of violation of the Persons With Disabilities Civil Rights Act, negligent supervision and intentional infliction of emotional distress.

Negligence claims brought by an employee against his/her employer are barred by the exclusive remedy provision of the Workers' Disability Compensation Act (WDCA). MCL 418.131 *Harris v Vernier*, 242 Mich App 306, 310-311 (2000). Accordingly, Defendant's motion for summary disposition of Plaintiff's negligent supervision claim is granted.

As to Plaintiff's emotional distress claim, four elements are necessary to make out a prima facie case of intentional infliction of emotional distress: extreme and outrageous conduct; intent or recklessness; causation; and severe emotional distress. *Roberts v AutoOwners Ins Co.*,

422 Mich 594 (1985). The test for liability for intentional infliction of emotional distress is whether the recitation of the facts to an average member of the community would arouse his resentment against the actor, and lead him to exclaim, "Outrageous!" *Graham v Ford*, 237 Mich App 670 (1999). Claims do not extend to mere insults or indignities.

Here, Plaintiff has failed to offer any evidence that Defendant's conduct was extreme and/or outrageous. Accordingly, Defendant's motion for summary disposition as to this count is granted.

As to Plaintiff's claim under the Persons With Disabilities Civil Rights claim, the Court finds that Plaintiff has not raised a genuine issue of material fact as to this claim and thus

Defendant's motion for summary disposition is granted.

Lastly, in order to establish a claim of hostile environment harassment, an employee must prove the following elements by a preponderance of the evidence:

(1) the employee belonged to a protected group;

(2) the employee was subjected to communication or conduct on the basis of his/her protected status;

(3) the employee was subjected to unwelcome conduct or communication involving the protected status;

(4) the unwelcome conduct or communication was intended to or in fact did substantially interfere with the employee's employment or created an intimidating, hostile, or offensive work environment; and

(5) respondeat superior. *Chambers v Trettco, Inc.,* 463 Mich 297 (2000) citing [*Radtke, supra* at 382-383, 501 N.W.2d 155,.

Here, Plaintiff has not established or alleged that she was subjected to communication or conduct that was based on her protected status as a female or an African American or that any unwelcome conduct related to her protected status created an intimidating, hostile or offensive workplace.

In addition, a plaintiff may prove a prima facie case of discrimination under the dissimilar treatment theory by showing that she is a member of a protected class and that she was treated differently than persona of a different class for the same or similar conduct. Here, although Plaintiff makes nonspecific allegations that a white female co-worker with MS was given preferential treatment but has not demonstrated that the special treatment was racially motivated. Plaintiff also complains of incidents involving her toolbox and locker. There has been no evidence presented that these incidents were due to Plaintiff's sex, race of MS. Plaintiff alleges that her supervisor made a remark regarding her MS prevented him from assigning her a specific job but there is no evidence that this was more than an isolated incident.

Accordingly, Defendant's motion for summary disposition as to Plaintiff's discrimination claims is also granted.

JOHN J. McDONALD

_____
JOHN J. McDONALD
CIRCUIT COURT JUDGE

CHAPTER 14

After I published a previous edition of this book, I received numerous answers to my questions about why my case did not get a fair court review, and so I decided to revise the book. My MS had become gradually worse. GM and I had reached an out of court "settlement" with Workers' Compensation. GM then breached the agreement and used administrative law judge, Melody Anne Paige, who I believe was very corrupt. She destroyed my out of court settlement with her lies. I thought it was important to let people see how a corrupt judge such as Paige and McDonald can ruin a case.

Richard Taylor had not filed my right-to-sue letter and I believe he had colluded with the GM attorney to throw my case. In my opinion, he was incompetent and crooked. I'd had reservations about him when I first met him and did not think he was intelligent enough to stand up to the GM attorney. Richard T. Taylor assured me that he was a capable attorney.

Some answers were not visible until years after the corrupt cases concluded in court. I filed charges against Mr. Taylor with the Attorney Grievance Commission of Michigan for ineffective representation, incompetence, collusion, and failure to file my appeal. He had not kept me informed of the status of my case; he had denied me the right to attend my own summary disposition hearings on four counts; he used the GM attorney's deposition that was missing 108 pages; he lied to me about filing my appeal; he hid my file in the bottom of his desk; and he failed to follow up on the right-to-sue letter from the EEOC. '

Judge McDonald had dismissed the racial discrimination, gender discrimination and disability discrimination charges against General Motors. Richard Taylor kept stringing me along until the statute of limitations for my case appeal had run out. Taylor stated to the Attorney Grievance Commission that I had written letters to the American Civil Liberties Union and other entities while my case was pending. This was false since he had already thrown my case before I wrote a letter to the ACLU.

Taylor stated that he knew nothing about my appeal. He wrote me a letter asking me if I wanted him to file my appeal. I sent the Attorney Grievance Commission a copy of the letter. Finally, he left the law firm and never informed me that he had not filed my appeal with the Michigan Court of Appeals.

Another plaintiff's case from the GM lawsuit went to a summary disposition hearing the same date and time as mine. Our hearings were scheduled together, and she was also told by Taylor that she could not attend the hearing. I spoke to one of the victims of the KKK outfit and he, too, was told he could not attend his summary disposition hearing by Taylor. A group leader had fashioned a white work robe into a KKK outfit and intimidated Black workers wearing it and no one was held accountable for this incident. Not one of us plaintiffs could attend summary disposition hearings according to Richard Taylor. I wrote to the ACLU on November 14, 2004, and gave my attorney a copy of the letter in which I complained about my treatment by the court. He should have told me at that time that he had not filed my appeal since there was still time to obtain another attorney. By failing to inform me, he had destroyed my chance to get justice.

The judge dismissed my case and sanctioned my co-plaintiff and me $3,000 each, the money being payable to GM's attorney. In Michigan the losing litigants pay the legal fees of the winning side, so GM received an extra bonus. The KKK victims were horrified when the judge threw out my case, and accepted the $5,000 GM offered them to prevent being sanctioned by the judge and risk paying GM. They knew I had received a right-to-sue letter from the Equal Employment Opportunity Commission for the gender harassment, and GM had admitted to discrimination against me because I am afflicted with Multiple Sclerosis. They had children to feed and could not afford such sanctions

Judge McDonald shut down 15 cases against GM with one swooping opinion. It was a fail-proof resolution to cover GM's negligence. General Motors was fully aware that minorities and women suffered abuse in the Pontiac Truck plant. It was the headline story of the "Detroit Free Press" on August 23, 2001. The attitudes of hourly and salaried employees were from the '50s, creating a very oppressive atmosphere for minority and female employees; and GM seemingly did nothing to discourage it in Pontiac. In fact GM seemed to exacerbate this and promote this terrorism. Judge John James McDonald allowed it to persist by ignoring the rule of law.

I don't believe attorney Taylor ever expected to see me again, but he was wrong and our paths happened to cross once again. My husband, daughter and I were headed to a benefit held in Ferndale, MI, July 29, 2004. As we were looking for a parking spot, a familiar face appeared in the parking lot.

I said to my husband, "Pull over. There's my attorney."

My husband pulled to the side, and Mr. Taylor peered in to see the driver.

I opened the window and said, "Hi, Mr. Taylor. This is my husband and my daughter."

"Hello, I'm just headed into this restaurant," he replied

"Did you file my appeal?"

He stammered, "I- I- I'm going to do it tomorrow."

"You told me you only had 21 days to file an appeal." He was still my attorney of record.

"I have 30 days after the judge enters his opinion. I still have time."

I looked at him in shocked disbelief and said, "30 days have passed since your letter"

"I still have time and will do it tomorrow."

"I will call you next week to check Mr. Taylor. File my appeal."

"I will do it first thing in the morning."

The following week after our conference in the parking lot, I called Mr. Taylor. It took me a few days to catch him but I did.

"Hi Mr. Taylor, it's Camille McMillan."

"Umm, hi."

"Did you file my appeal?"

"Yes, I filed it a couple of days ago."

"You were able to file it."

"Yes, I told you I could and I did it."

"What do I do now?"

"Sit back and wait until the appeal comes up. I'll notify you when that happens."

"Thank you. What about the sanctions? When and where do I pay them?"

"You don't have to worry about them. You only pay if you lose on appeal."

"Oh, I didn't know that. Thanks."

The last time I saw attorney Taylor in his office, he showed me one page of the deposition. It merely contained the statement that the latest supervisors to join in the harassment were Black. I was puzzled as to why he thought that reduced the responsibility of the company for racial discrimination in the plant. Everyone knows that trick. You get the supervisors of the same race as the victim to continue the harassment. They still were GM managers and still men who were threatening and harassing me on behalf of the management while hoping to get promotions.

Richard Taylor claimed to be a "Civil Rights" attorney, and as a Black man, himself, he should have known the tricks. Instead he seemed to operate more as the company's advocate. He clutched my deposition tightly in his fist and would not allow me to view any more pages or look through it. If he had, I would have noticed the missing pages and the fact that it was an obviously Xeroxed copy.

I did as he instructed, and sat back, and waited. I am a layman in the ways of the legal world and was as naive as I could be. I actually thought that Taylor was looking out for my interests. Many have asked why I didn't reach out for more help. I wrote letters to the NAACP Detroit, NAACP Oakland County, NAACP National, the ACLU, my elected Congressman and Senators, the Governor, the Lieutenant Governor and Attorney General, as well as to Jesse Jackson and Al Sharpton. None of them represented me, I talked to my State Representative and wrote to both The Detroit Free Press and to USA Today, which had featured in an article about whistle-blowers another female electrician from my plant who had suffered abuse. I wrote to the U.S. Department of Justice Civil Rights Division, who referred me back to the investigator who issued me the right-to-sue letter, and to just about anyone who should listen. The agent from the EEOC was as surprised as I that the judge had thrown out my case. Only later did I learn that Richard Taylor had never filed my right-to-sue letter from the EEOC.

I got no response from most of the Civil Rights groups, and only form letters from the elected officials explaining why they couldn't get involved but they wanted donations. Self-proclaimed Civil Rights leaders and advocates who were accepting money from General Motors didn't want to fall off their *gravy train,* and remained silent.

I visited to the Bloomfield Associates where attorney Taylor had done half the work on my case. I called the original attorney, H. Wallace Parker and scheduled a meeting. He cancelled it and we had to reschedule. On March 16, 2006 we had our meeting.

Attorney Lewis looked at me and said, "There's nothing in your file indicating an appeal was filed on your behalf."

I shivered as he continued, "I found your file stuffed in the bottom of his old desk. I thought he had taken it with him to work on your case."

I replied, "He told me I wouldn't have to pay the sanctions unless I lost on appeal."

"No, that's not true. I was walking by his office and heard him say to someone on the phone, "I won't file her appeal if you don't go after her for the sanctions. I didn't know who he was talking about."

My blood ran cold. I had been subjected to nightmarish treatment at General Motors, and my attorney had pulled a Benedict Arnold on me and failed to file my appeal. I wanted some records from my legal file for my book that I was preparing for the Court of Public opinion. Attorney Lewis allowed me to take the file home. What I saw when I researched it was eye popping.

In the meantime, I was forced to retire on disability, my health was deteriorating, and I was fighting GM for Workers' Comp. Judge McDonald stated that this was the only form of redress I had. McDonald knew I had filed a Workers' Compensation claim. GM's attorney, Alex Alexopolous, was a legal hit man in my opinion and asked me about it in my deposition as if he were trying that case also. A lot of the questions he asked seemed to pertain to the Worker's Comp case which had not yet been to court. He kept referring to Dr. Dvorkin as "mister," showing that he had no respect for him.

GM decision makers had pulled every trick in the book to keep me from getting my Workers' Compensation case to trial. They changed attorneys numerous times (sometimes in the same law office) and subjected me to repeat visits to *their* doctors.

Their psychiatrist violated the privacy between my psychologist and me. During the interview proceedings, he violated the HIPAA (Health Insurance Portability and Accountability Act), which was designed to protect patients' privacy and the confidentiality of their medical records.

"Give me a conversation between you and Dr. Dvorkin." I stared at him in shock. I didn't know what to say. He had no right to ask that.

"Come on, come on. What do you two talk about when you are with him? Give me a typical conversation."

I couldn't respond. He was responsible for writing his own report, not taking a private conversation between me and my doctor and then writing a report to counter what I had said to my doctor. He later wrote that I could not answer his questions when he asked what Dr. Dvorkin had done for me. I was in shock from his invasion of my privacy. He sat back in his chair and put his foot on his desk, his foot blocking my face to show his disrespect for me.

Attorney Taylor showed up at the law firm after another attorney handling the GM cases left in 2003. The original case was filed in 2002. That attorney had told me he was leaving and possibly would be working for GM. Attorney Taylor had taken over from him. I asked Taylor if he had time to depose GM management. He assured me he had the time. There was one attorney, Taylor, handling numerous lawsuits against GM. All the cases were controlled by Judge John J. McDonald and he dismissed them one by one.

Attorney Taylor never even deposed one GM manager. I had witnesses willing to testify on my behalf who either called the law firm or physically appeared at the Law office on my behalf in 2003. Attorney Taylor seemed to have made his mind up that he would get me to settle for $4,500 before my case went to the summary disposition hearing and mediation. In the file Taylor left behind I found letters addressed to me that he had written three months after he was on the job, encouraging me to settle for $4,500 which he never sent.

Many of the other plaintiffs were upset with him for pressuring them to settle for $4,500. Judge McDonald sanctioned another Black woman and me $3,000 each. Our cases were presented together in front of Judge John James McDonald for summary disposition. Hence, the quid pro quo (Something for something). She paid. I didn't. GM garnisheed her check because Attorney Taylor never informed her where to pay her sanctions. The other plaintiff told me Attorney Taylor sent her to talk to GM's attorney herself.

She filed charges against attorney Taylor too. The Attorney Grievance Commission dismissed her complaint. She never received a written opinion of the proceedings either. I never paid the sanctions and I received a written opinion from judge John James McDonald.

My deposition was scheduled by GM on December 22, 2003. Attorney Taylor called me to tell me that it had been cancelled. S.J. Bashen called my house at least seven times to talk to me about the charges I had filed with the Michigan Department of Civil Rights. I'd made it clear that I would never talk to them again without counsel. S.J. Bashen was trying to bypass the MDCR (Michigan Department of Civil Rights). MDCR later switched the case to the EEOC, which is under federal jurisdiction. I also called Mr. Taylor, who told me to ask S.J. Bashen to call him. S.J. Bashen insisted on meeting with me, alone. I was having none of that, and referred them to Mr. Taylor. They were not pleased. GM had previously paid this Black-owned firm to represent them in my case three years earlier with Ms. Moss. I would not trust them again.

The deposition for my case with judge McDonald was rescheduled for Jan 5, 2004. I waited for Richard Taylor for well over an hour in the lobby of GM's law firm, Hardy Lewis & Page. He never arrived. Richard Taylor's law firm sent another lawyer to replace him when it became apparent that Taylor was not going to show. Civil Rights was not this lawyer's area of practice, but she did what she could.

GM's attorney, Alex Alexopolous, questioned why I had cancelled the last deposition. I hadn't cancelled the deposition; Richard Taylor had. GM's attorney was also not pleased that I'd refused to speak with S.J. Bashen about the Michigan Department of Civil Rights case because of my prior experience with them.

It was apparent that GM's attorney was used to intimidating and tormenting complainants. During the deposition I sat under bright lights as he asked me personal questions that had no bearing on my case.

GM's attorney sought from the start to discredit me. The first items he asked for in the interrogatories were my tax records, police records, and school transcripts. I pay my taxes, was high school valedictorian and class president, have never been arrested, had an excellent credit score, and do community service. I don't believe the GM attorney thought I could overcome the credibility problem many people face these days. As a Black American, I would have been expected to fail on at least one or two these points. I didn't. I held up under the GM attorney Alex Alexopolous' relentless grilling and made steady eye contact with him. If my MS worsened, it would not be with me cowering and begging for his mercy. He was ruthless. He was also very intelligent. Mr. Alexopolous tried to destroy my marriage.

He looked at me and said, "Did your husband tell you that he was going to divorce you?

" What?"

" Did your husband tell you he was going to divorce you?

He leaned in and looked at me as if he knew this to be true.

"No."

The GM attorney was willing to destroy my family in order to save GM. I just shook my head because I knew better. I don't think either Richard Taylor or the judge had the mental capacity to deal with Alex. It was easier for them to roll over.

I had to face the fact that Taylor had violated my trust, and I wondered what he had gotten out of it. I honestly believe he was brought in to destroy all the cases against GM. He did a great job not representing his clients. The Independent Medical Exam with GM's psychiatrist was a joke. The exam is paid for by GM and the doctors normally favor those who pay them.

The so-called doctor began asking me questions about my MS. He asked me, "How many days have you missed work because of the MS?" When I replied, "None," his face fell. I worked 12-16 hours a day, seven days a week. He figured that if I missed a lot of time, he could blame my work problems on my MS. Since he was being paid by GM his job was to get the company off even if he had to lie. He started asking me if I went to church. What did my religion have to do with this exam? He went to church but it didn't stop him from bearing false witness against me.

The Independent Medical Exam with the GM neurologist went the same way. He had wanted to conduct an EMG (Electromyogram) on me. In this procedure the patient is stabbed with needles and given electric shocks controlled by the doctor to gauge your nerve and muscle reaction. Since the doctor controls the amps or the flow of current, he can make the test extremely painful. The higher the amps, the more the pain. You are being electrocuted. I had been through two of these tests and they were extremely painful. There was actually no need for the test since it had already been determined that I had MS. I thought it was another way to torture me. My neurologist said that the test wasn't needed and I didn't take the test.

A friend told me about the Attorney Grievance Commission, a Michigan State Government agency charged with maintaining the integrity and credibility of the justice system by weeding out incompetent or crooked attorneys. I decided to try to bring charges against my attorney. On April 7, 2006, I filed charges against Attorney Taylor. I told the Attorney Grievance Commission that he did not file my appeal, did not keep me informed of the progress of my case, denied me the right to be in the court, would not tell me when my case went before the judge, and intentionally threw my case.

The Attorney Grievance Commission sent me a letter acknowledging receipt of my complaint and sent Attorney Taylor a copy for his response. Taylor denied any knowledge of my appeal. He stated that his involvement had ended at the summary disposition and that it was the responsibility of the law firm to pursue my appeal. His dates for the summary disposition and when I contacted other agencies were off, some by years. In my file I found a letter addressed to me stating we'd had a meeting during which he had explained everything to me. The letter was never sent. Attorney Parker told me that he had to remove some items from the file before he gave it to me. I have no idea of the documents he removed. The meeting was in Taylor's mind only, and we never did discuss what he claimed in the letter. He claimed that he tried to get GM to settle with me for 30 years and out. His letter stated that he was trying to get GM to allow me to retire and pay me as if I had 30 years seniority.

It was back and forth with the Attorney Grievance Commission as the administrative case stalled. The AGC had the case for almost two years! Attorney Taylor negotiated his own deal. The Attorney Discipline Board decided to accept his negotiation and he was allowed to continue practicing law. However, he did received a reprimand on April 1, 2008. He threw my case, and all he received was a written reprimand and a small fine of $900 which went to the AGC while I had to leave my job and suffer even more as the MS worsened. Taylor was issued another reprimand July 12, 2017.

Where was the justice? My union was no better. Whenever I asked for assistance from my union I got none. The union was upset that I would not go along with their allowing other electricians to use and abuse me. The union felt I should otherwise shut up and protect the guys who were doing all of the wrongs.

One committeeman told me that I should go along with the program. A plant chairman asked me to write more grievances against GM. When I refused he started yelling at me that he needed these grievances written.

One of the grievances he wanted me to write was about the dangerous conditions of the line cells. They were loaded with weld slag, which made the cells slippery and dangerous. I refused. He was a big guy, and he stood over me yelling and trying to intimidate me into writing the grievance. If I had written it, the union would not have protected me again from the backlash of the company. I was a lone woman working around hundreds of men. I had to stand my ground and not allow any of them to use me. If I had let one of them use me that would have opened up the floodgates for all of them to use me, and I had many of them trying. If I had slept with Derek, others would follow. They would try to pass me amongst themselves and that wasn't going to happen. That is part of plant life. A lot of the men are beast.

The union assisted management in harassing me like the incident earlier with Amos Horace at the MIG welder. Amos and my committeeman were setting me up for discipline at the MIG welder I believe, but I caught them. The union refused to write my grievances, refused to help me get the pay I was denied, and settled the few grievances I did write in favor of the company. My union officials (all men) cussed at me instead whenever I called them.

My tormentor, Chad, became friends with a union official's son, Michael Dandridge. Michael and I had worked together at American Axle. No one liked him because of his father. They felt his father had sold out the Skilled Trades workers by not negotiating a fair contract for tradesmen. His father got him hired at American Axle. Chad seized the opportunity to befriend him because Chad is an opportunist. When Michael got to Pontiac he received special treatment. He was responsible for making water cannons and shooting people with them at work. The cannons knocked people to the floor. Michael introduced Chad into the UAW. Chad only had two years with the UAW and rose swiftly through the International ranks. They promoted and protected a thief who was harassing and threatening a female employee. I asked Derek what Michael said after Derek broke his hand hitting the cabinet above my head. Derek said, "He wants to hit you with the water cannon. It had come to that. Michael was no longer my friend and had become a good ole boy.

Derek told management that he had tried to punch me out. He thought all the management loved him. When management threatened to fire him, he became scared and started telling people that I had told on him. I had never said a word. Management hated me more than they loved Derek. Derek had told on himself and Michael wanted to shoot me with the water cannon. He didn't care that I have MS, and Derek didn't care about putting my life in danger.

My first eight weeks off work, General Motors refused to pay me medical pay or my medical bills because I had left for mental abuse and not physical. GM's reasoning was that the psychologist who removed me from the hostile and volatile work environment was not a medical doctor, and therefore not qualified to make the call for removal. Dr. Dvorkin was not qualified to remove me from a hostile volatile work environment, but if I had threatened to harm anyone under state laws, he would have had a duty to report it.

GM stalled my Workers Comp case by changing attorneys. Sometimes the attorneys worked in the same law firm. My Workers Compensation attorney had to re-file the case in early 2005 because of an error he made. GM began the stalling game again by the switching of attorneys, sometimes rotating the same ones back and forth. GM must have changed attorneys about 15 times. When a new Michigan Governor was elected, the magistrate handling my case was replaced. GM immediately sent me back to their doctors for re-evaluation after the new Governor, Rick Snyder, was elected. GM already had their chance, but they subjected me to double evaluations in order to get the report they wanted. GM seems to rule Michigan.

October 15, 2007, was my scheduled court date for worker's comp. Days before court, I reached an out-of-court settlement with GM on the Workers' Comp issue. The law firm of Lacey & Jones, in Birmingham, MI, handled the settlement for GM. Jan 30, 2008 was set by the Board of Work Compensation as a court redemption date, the date they were going to disburse my Workers' Compensation settlement. One of the settlement conditions was that I needed a Medicare set-aside letter proving I had alternate insurance as well as stipulations of the settlement that concerned Medicare. In the set aside letter GM agreed to put aside so much money for my medical needs. In my case they agreed to set aside $10,000. I didn't know all the stipulations for Medicare because GM never applied for the letter and GM had agreed to take care of all the necessary paperwork.

On January 29, 2008, my attorney called me to say the Medicare set-aside letter had not arrived and there would be no court date. The next redemption date was set for April 28, 2008. I heard nothing concerning the letter, and a 90-day ordeal was quickly turning into a 120-day ordeal. I called my attorney in the middle of March to see what the hold-up was. Again, no letter. I started calling Medicare myself. When I finally reached a live person, I was informed that no one had requested a letter on my behalf.

This request was not in Medicare's system. I informed my Worker's Comp attorney, who went to work on it. We spoke of the options, but I smelled the stench of stall tactics in the wind, and determined it would be best to proceed to trial for a judge to settle the case. GM began to pay Dr. Dvorkin as part of the settlement agreement. Besides agreeing to send for the Medicare set-aside letter, GM had agreed to pay me $150,000for the mental harassment (one can only get so much per year with work comp), pay to set up Medicare set-aside account, and fund the amount Medicare assessed for my future mental health care. They also agreed to reimburse me the $10,000 dollars I paid Dr. Dvorkin out of my own pocket. It was reimbursement my insurance should have otherwise paid and didn't. Nonetheless General Motors had done nothing. There was a reason why. GM was playing games.

After cancelling the redemption date of April 28, 2008 due to GM breaching the out of court settlement, my case was slated to continue on to trial. Magistrate Melody Paige told my attorney that if she made GM adhere to the out of court settlement GM would immediately appeal it and stall my case for years, although she controlled the timeline. The GM attorney informed my attorney that the GM attorney who settled my case for GM (their agent from Lacey & Jones, (Richard D. Lovernick), did not have the authority to settle with me for the agreed-upon amount. Therefore, GM would be willing to settle with me at this hearing, but for one-third less than the amount stipulated in the agreement. They imposed the additional condition that I never speak of what happened to me. It would permanently close my case.

GM had bargained in bad faith. Bad faith bargaining is committing an "intentional dishonest act by not fulfilling legal or contractual obligations, misleading another, entering into an agreement without the intention or means to fulfill or violating basic standards of honesty in dealing with others." I therefore rejected GM's offer and decided to continue to trial. The attorney Richard D. Lovernick was representing GM's interest at the time.

If GM had an issue with the settlement, then they should have gotten the money from Lacey & Jones who oversaw the settlement and whose attorney made the deceptive agreement. I would have gone to court Oct. 15, 2007 and closed this chapter of my life. It was another stall tactic and they had no intentions of living up to their agreements.

The next court dates were August 27 and September 4, 2008, even though GM and I had already reached an out of court settlement on Oct. 15, 2007, a settlement which GM had intentionally breached. Magistrate Paige's first instruction to me that I could not fully comprehend was that I couldn't tell her what was said directly to me by any GM managers. She barred some of my testimony and I didn't understand that. GM could then bring in the managers to refute what I was saying. I understand now that these managers would be subject to cross examination and some were not too bright.

I knew at the outset of the trial that I would not receive justice. I knew Ms. Paige would do anything to let GM off the hook. I did not have *hearsay* evidence. This was exactly what was said to me. I had direct evidence that Ms. Paige would not allow me to testify about. GM produced none of the managers that I named as bullies. In Worker's Comp hearings the defendant produces the witnesses. I believe this was the start of her corruption of my evidence.

To: Mike 1 Smith/US/GM/GMC@GM
cc: Michael Southwell/US/GM/GMC@GM
Subject: Conditioning Line Incident

On Wednesday, May 8, 2002 at approximately 9:10am, I was walking south along conditioning Line #1 and noticed an extension cord tied in the shape of a "noose" above the ventilation duct on the west side of Conditioning Line #2 at approximately E-42. Upon seeing the cord wrapped in that fashion, I looked around to see if anyone was observing me standing near the cord. I saw no one in the immediate vicinity. The cord was suspened from the overhead steel and wrapped around conduit and plugged into a receptacle. I could not dislodge the cord from the receptacle and did not want to draw too much attention to myself. I then untied the noose and set the cord [untied] back upon the top of the ventilation duct. At that point I radioed Final Superintendent Mike Smith and let him know what I found and where I found it. Mike then contacted Personnel and I joined Mike in his office when Personnel Staff came to his location.

Any questions, please contact me at 2451.

SAS

CAMILLE MCMILLAN

12.   Conditioning Line Incident Report

Plaintiff wrote a letter to Mike Smith indicating that on May 8, 2002, she was walking when she noticed an extension cord tied in the shape of a "noose" above the ventilation duct on the west side of Conditioning Line #2. Plaintiff untied the noose and reported it to Mr. Smith.

13.   Employee Grievance

Plaintiff filed two grievances. January 30, 2003, claiming that Verlynn Matthews had reset Robot Faults at BS3 twice. It appears that this was outside the bargaining unit work. On February 3, 2003, plaintiff charged management with creating hostile working conditions and harassment. Verlyn Matthews was reported to be doing plaintiff's work and constantly harassing her. Both grievances were "No Caused"

DEFENDANT

A.   Dr. Gerald Robbins, D.O

The doctor is board certified in Neurology (R p 4). The doctor has spoken with the plaintiff on three different occasions; the first was May 10, 2004, (R p 11) for an Independent Medical Exam (R p 13). Plaintiff reported having stopped work in 2003 because of her multiple sclerosis and stress (R p 14). Plaintiff exhibited some abnormal neurological responses and in view of the fact that she does relate working at heights, climbing, lifting and bending, the doctor would not recommend that she return to her job duties as an electrician until he reviewed the latest MRI results (R p 17).

On July 25, 2006, the doctor re-examined the plaintiff. Plaintiff reported increased symptoms of MS and was using a cane (R p 20). The plaintiff refused to undergo a physical exam and refused to give permission for the doctor to request medical records (R p 21). The physical symptoms that the plaintiff was reporting were consistent with MS which is considered a non-occupational condition (R p 22).

Plaintiff was again seen on November 7, 2006. The plaintiff was found to be unable to do any type of gainful employment (R p 28). Plaintiff has Multiple Sclerosis with multiple areas of scarring of the white matter of the nervous system, the brain, and the spinal cord as well as some of the nerves (R p 30). It is a disorder where the nervous system has events where the myelin, the white covering of the nerves in the brain and spinal cord become inflamed and do not function properly during an exacerbation. The person might have problems with

12

Memorandum

To: File No: 65268-10LL

CC: [Click here and type name]

From: Lorenzo A. D'Agostini

Date: October 30, 2007

Re: Camille McMillian

We agreed to settle this case for $150,000.00 plus defendants would waive any LTD/S&A pay back and they have agreed to pay up to $10,000.00 towards any Medicare Set-Aside. Additionally, they will hire and pay for a company to do the set aside proposal. I confirmed all this by telephone with Mr. Lovernick on the morning of October 15, 2007.

LAD/smd

1

LAW OFFICES
LEVINE, BENJAMIN, TUSHMAN, BRATT,
JERRIS AND STEIN, P.C.
27700 NORTHWESTERN HIGHWAY
100 GALLERIA OFFICENTRE, SUITE 411
SOUTHFIELD, MICHIGAN 48034

(248) 352-5700
FAX (248) 352-1312

LORENZO A. D'AGOSTINI

FLINT
PETOSKEY

October 30, 2007

Camille McMillian
6649 Westwood Court, #40-205
West Bloomfield, MI 48322

   RE: Worker's Compensation Claim
     Our File No: 65268-10LL

Dear Ms. McMillian:

   Please be advised that the Bureau of Workers' Disability Compensation has set a Redemption Date of **January 30, 2008 at 9:00 a.m.**

   Please make arrangements to meet me at the Bureau of Workers' Disability Compensation, Bank One Building, 28 N. Saginaw, Suite 1310, Pontiac, Michigan at **8:45 a.m.** on **January 30, 2008.**

   If you should have any questions, please do not hesitate to contact me at your convenience.

      Very truly yours,

      LEVINE, BENJAMIN, TUSHMAN,
      BRATT, JERRIS and STEIN, P.C.

      Lorenzo A. D'Agostini

LAD/smc

February 12, 2008

Richard N. Lovernick, Esq.
LACEY & JONES
Suite 525
City Center Building
220 East Huron
Ann Arbor, MI 48104

      RE: Camille F. McMillian vs General Motors
            Our File No: 65268-10LL

Dear Mr. Lovernick:

Please be advised that the above entitled matter has been scheduled for a Redemption Date of April 30, 2008 at 9:00 a.m. at the Pontiac Bureau of Workers' Disability Compensation.

Please mark your calendar accordingly.

             Very truly yours,

             LEVINE, BENJAMIN, TUSHMAN,
             BRATT, JERRIS & STEIN, P.C.

             Lorenzo A. D'Agostini

LAD/smc

202

In my opinion Not a very good doctor

CAMILLE MCMILLAN

GM doctor Dr. Mercier who is Board Certified in Psychiatry, testified that it was his opinion that the plaintiff's multiple sclerosis was affecting the emotional part of her brain, namely the limbic system. The doctor felt that the plaintiff might have an organic affective disorder which was a psychiatric condition in which there is a physical basis for an alteration of mood, it was not a condition that was caused by interpersonal friction or conflict. The plaintiff's examination did not support plaintiff's allegation that she suffered a significant psychiatric illness in the work place. It was this doctor's opinion that from a psychiatric perspective plaintiff was not limited or restricted in any fashion. The doctor did not think that the stressors plaintiff could be experiencing at work would worsen or trigger the MS; I found this reasoning to be sound and convincing and this theory is hereby adopted by this authority.

Disability, Sington v Chrysler Corp, 467 Mich 144; 648 NW2d 624 (2002), Analysis

It is agreed with the medical authorities that have testified in this matter that plaintiff is disabled from any and all employment that she may have had the qualifications and training to do in her younger years. However, it is found that this disability is the result of the natural progression of the disease Multiple Sclerosis and therefore not the result of any work related indent and not compensable under the act.

Rakestraw v General Dynamics Land Systems, 469 Mich 220; 666 NW2d 199 (2003), Analysis:

Although plaintiff underlying pathology has changed and evolved over the years this change is in no way related to her employment with General Motors.

Ms. paige ignored every thing my doctors had to say.

ORDER

IT IS HEREBY ORDERED THAT benefits are denied.

WORKERS' COMPENSATION BOARD OF MAGISTRATES

MELODY PAIGE, Magistrate (195)

Signed this 16th day of April 2009, at Pontiac, Michigan.

18

203

JENNIFER M. GRANHOLM
GOVERNOR

STATE OF MICHIGAN
DEPARTMENT OF CIVIL RIGHTS
DETROIT

NANETTE LEE REYNOLDS, Ed. D.
DIRECTOR

September 25, 2003

Mrs. Camille McMillan
14530 Balfour
Oak Park, MI 48237

RE : MDCR Contact #   311006 Camille McMillan v General Motors Corporation

Dear Mrs. McMillan:

On September 3, 2003, you contacted the Michigan Department of Civil Rights about the above matter. In order to continue the processing of your concern you must submit the following required information to the department by October 2, 2003:

The respondent has expressed an interest in the early resolution process. I need to speak with you as soon as possible regarding your claim.

If the department does not receive the requested information by October 2, 2003, the department will discontinue processing your concern.

If you have questions, please contact me immediately.

Sincerely,

V. Stacy Cobb
Rights Representative
phone: 313-456-3771
fax: 313-456-3781
email: cobbv@michigan.gov

- 3700 D talk to her directly

never talked to my Rep during investigation

EEOC Form 161 (10/96)

U.S. EQUAL EMPLOYMENT OPPORTUNITY COMMISSION

DISMISSAL AND NOTICE OF RIGHTS

To: Camille McMillan 14530 Balfour Oak Park, MI 48237	From: U. S. Equal Employment Opportunity Commission Room 865; Patrick V. McNamara Building 477 Michigan Avenue Detroit, Michigan 48226

[ ] *On behalf of person(s) aggrieved whose identity is*
CONFIDENTIAL (29 CFR § 1601.7(a))

Charge No.	EEOC Representative	Telephone No.
23A-2004-00092	Spyridon E. Melios, Investigator	(313) 226-4629

THE EEOC IS CLOSING ITS FILE ON THIS CHARGE FOR THE FOLLOWING REASON:

[ ] The facts alleged in the charge fail to state a claim under any of the statutes enforced by the EEOC.

[ ] Your allegations did not involve a disability that is covered by the Americans with Disabilities Act.

[ ] The Respondent employs less than the required number of employees or is not otherwise covered by the statutes.

[ ] We cannot investigate your charge because it was not filed within the time limit required by law.

[ ] Having been given 30 days in which to respond, you failed to provide information, failed to appear or be available for interviews/conferences, or otherwise failed to cooperate to the extent that it was not possible to resolve your charge.

[ ] While reasonable efforts were made to locate you, we were not able to do so.

[ ] You had 30 days to accept a reasonable settlement offer that affords full relief for the harm you alleged.

[X] The EEOC issues the following determination: Based upon its investigation, the EEOC is unable to conclude that the information obtained establishes violations of the statutes. This does not certify that the respondent is in compliance with the statutes. No finding is made as to any other issues that might be construed as having been raised by this charge.

[ ] The EEOC has adopted the findings of the state or local fair employment practices agency that investigated this charge.

[ ] Other *(briefly state)* _____

- NOTICE OF SUIT RIGHTS -
(See the additional information attached to this form.)

Title VII, the Americans with Disabilities Act, and/or the Age Discrimination in Employment Act: This will be the only notice of dismissal and of your right to sue that we will send you. You may file a lawsuit against the respondent(s) under federal law based on this charge in federal or state court. Your lawsuit must be filed **WITHIN 90 DAYS** from your receipt of this Notice; otherwise, your right to sue based on this charge will be lost. (The time limit for filing suit based on a state claim may be different.)

Equal Pay Act (EPA): EPA suits must be filed in federal or state court within 2 years (3 years for willful violations) of the alleged EPA underpayment. This means that backpay due for any violations that occurred **more than 2 years (3 years)** before you file suit may not be collectible.

On behalf of the Commission

James R. Neely, Jr., Director   2/24/04

(Date Mailed)

Enclosure(s)

cc: General Motors Corporation

205

S.J. Bashen does work for the EEOC

Camille F. McMillan Briefing

Background

On May 25, 2001, Pontiac East Assembly (John Myers, Personnel Director) received a copy of the Camille McMillan letter dated May 18, 2001, to Gerald A. Knechtel depicting several allegations of harassment and discrimination in the Body Shop. Camille McMillan is an African American female, journeyperson Electrician assigned to the Pontiac East Body Shop. Camille's GM Seniority Date is 08-02-76, Plant Seniority Date 01-07-85, and GM Skill Date 12-13-93. The first incident of alleged harassment was by her male co-workers which involved movement of her Toolbox in the November 1999 timeframe. Followed by co-workers posting a harassing picture of "roadkill" in her work area. The most recent allegation stated in her letter (May 18, 2001) are several points specific to favoritism regarding vacation approvals and job assignment selections within the Pontiac East Body Shop.

Actions Taken

Upon receipt of the Camille McMillan letter, Pontiac East Personnel Department reacted immediately to the stated allegations by initiating a comprehensive investigation process on May 25, 2001. S.J. Bashen Corporation was contacted (suggested by Corporate Employee Relations Staff) to conduct an immediate investigation of the allegations brought forth by Camille McMillan. Cheryl ▆▆▆ was assigned to the investigation from S.J. Bashen Corporation. Cheryl arrived on the next business day Tuesday, May 29, 2001, (5-28-01 was Memorial Day) to begin the investigation. In addition, the Pontiac East Personnel Department contacted the UAW Local 594 Civil Rights Representative (▆▆ ▆▆▆) to investigate into Camille's allegations in conjunction with Management. ▆▆▆▆▆ (UAW Local 594 Civil Rights Representative) stated on May 30, 2001 that he had been contacted directly by Camille on April 4, 2001, and conducted an investigation with her on April 9, 2001, with respect to the same points named in the May 18, 2001, formal letter, however he was not able to substantiate a National Agreement Paragraph 6(a) violation (Discrimination) for lack of evidence warranting a grievance.

Camille McMillan was out of Pontiac East on vacation the dates of May 25 and May 29, 2001. The investigation into the allegations began on May 29, 2001 and concluded after speaking to the final person on May 30, 2001.

S.J. Bashen (▆▆▆ Brown) Concluding Briefing

- With respect to the 1999 Toolbox incident, ▆▆ Brown recommended that it is in the best interest of Management not to focus the investigation on this alleged incident for several reasons:
  - The time limitations have expired to file Federal or State charges.

UIM001 L 01/04

EMPLOYEE GRIEVANCE No.G 0029

Dept. _4461_ Date _2-22-02_ Time _9:29_ A.M.

Nature of Grievance _I CHARGE MGMT WITH_
VIO. OF N.A. PAR 202 LMSA. AND
SETTLED GRIEV.# F4563. I WAS DENIED
VAC. TIME OF IN JUNE BECAUSE OF
PARTIAL MIK. THIS IS FAVORABLY IN
BAD FAITH. I DEMAND TO BE MADE
WHOLE & THIS PRACTICE STOP.

Signed _____

Committeeman _____ SS# / Clock No. _390-70-7325_

Reported to _____ Foreman

Disposition by Foreman

MGT. WILL PAY 26.00 by
PAR. 202 OF the NAT. AND
_GRIEV F4563. ___ K. W____ 11°/Am_

Date _7-23-02_ _____

Disposition by _____

Disposition by _Management in writing_
is that the next week will
the priority over a
partime worker

Date _7-23-02_

Grievance Satisfactorily Settled | Referred to Management Shop Committee Meeting

_No 3 M___

Disposition By Management
No Comment
verify to worker rel. 5-21-02

Date _____ Signed _____

Grievance Satisfactorily Settled | Appealed

_No / 5M___

→ Violation of National Agreement

CHAPTER 15

One strong desire I had for a long time was to study Judaism. I found what I was searching for while I began to studying Judaism and entered a new world.

I really wanted to study Judaism. One must study the faith before one can convert. Once at his office I said to Dr. Dvorkin, "I know you know somewhere where I can at least take classes." He stared at me with penetrating eyes. A few weeks went by and I continued to press him. I was serious. I just wanted the opportunity to take classes and decide for myself what was right for me. At my next appointment with Dr. Dvorkin, I noticed a green card on his desk. As our session ended, he picked it up and looked at me.

"You've been asking me about Judaism classes for some time."

"Yes, I have," My heart raced with anticipation.

"You know I don't care any way about what you do with religion."

"Yes, I know, but I have been bugging you. I just want the opportunity to take classes and decide. I am really interested."

He stared at me and slid me the card. It was a card advertising the Introduction to Judaism class held at Temple Israel beginning the following week. My heart raced and I hurried home to sign up. I was hoping it was not too late. When I arrived home I immediately placed the phone call to sign up. I was thrilled I was not too late. My daughter arrived home soon and I told her my good news.

"I wanted to take the class with you," she said.

"I'm sorry, I can call back and try to add you. It may not be too late. I didn't realize how serious you were. I wanted to make sure that I had no impact on your decision and I would respect your decision. It's your life."

I made the conversion official on Oct. 24, 2006. We began living new lives. We had Shabbat dinner every Friday evening and then proceeded to *Service*. I began learning Hebrew. It is an interesting language. The Detroit Jewish News ran a story on people converting to Judaism. There were articles on different families or individuals who converted. They ran a story on my family. Surprisingly we were the cover story for the magazine that week. The week of December 21, 2006, a friend called my daughter and told her he saw us on the cover of the Jewish News. We thought he was kidding. He loved practical jokes and the magazine was not due to hit the newsstands yet. Later she went to the store and home.

"Mom, Mom," she yelled as she ran up the steps.

"I'm coming, what's wrong?"

"Look, we are on the cover of the Jewish News."

"You're kidding me, right?"

"No mom, look!" as she thrust the paper at me excitedly.

I was shocked. I never expected to make the cover of any magazine, and least of all the Jewish News. What a wonderful "welcome to the community" gift. We purchased 25 copies and sent them to friends and relatives.

One dark cloud tried to steal my joy. I began receiving phone calls early Friday morning, December 22, 2006. Everyone was calling to inform me that my stalker and harasser, Stan Minard, had died while on company time. Apparently, he left the job during working hours, visited his girl-friend, and overdosed on cocaine. His heart gave out. Some asked that I forgive him for what he put me through, right then. Of course, they hadn't gone through stalking, death threats, and constant fear every day because of his violent behavior. They didn't have to live with the damage he helped inflict on my body. I felt for his family, losing one they loved; but I hadn't wished him any physical harm, nor did I hate him. My conscience was clear and I could move on with my life.

Dr. Leuchter, my Neurologist, wanted me to try physical therapy first to see if I could build up muscle strength. My therapist was wonderful. My legs were weakening and my balance shot. My mobility was now threatened with having to have assistance. I was already using a cane, a scooter, and wheelchairs. We worked on the muscle groups to keep me upright. My mobility became compromised, just as I feared when I approached GM management to plead with them to intervene and halt the harassment.

Since my civil case had been destroyed by Judge John James McDonald and my corrupt attorney, Richard Terrell Taylor, I still had hope in my Workers Compensation case. I actually believed I would find an honest magistrate.

I left work Oct. 17, 2003, and filed my Workers Compensation case about one month later. My attorney made an error and the case had to be re-filed in May of 2005. After I left, the Queen retired also. She took a job with the robot company that trained her. Her attitude didn't change and they released her.

On August 27, 2008, I finally entered Magistrate Melody Anne Paige's courtroom. She had sent us home numerous times when we reported for the hearing. We were never told why she wasn't hearing my case on those days. One time I was the only one in the lobby when she exited for lunch. I was sitting there crocheting, minding my own business. When she saw me she stopped dead in her tracks. The way she looked at me told me she didn't know what to do with me. I had clearly unnerved her.

My husband and I entered the courtroom. He took a seat in the last row by himself since he was not a witness. We started the hearing with issues that were not under dispute. GM had no problems with these items. We went back and forth on issues that were easy to resolve. The hard stuff was for the magistrate to decide. After about an hour we adjourned until the next week.

When I finally sat down in the witness chair, the only people present were the two attorneys, my husband, the judge, and me. As the trial began, the magistrate, Melody Anne Paige immediately insulted my husband. She looked at him with disdain as she sneered at him, "Sir, do you work?" I was shocked because his working had nothing to do with my case. My husband has a degree, and yes, he works. He has worked for the State of Michigan over 25 years. I would never marry a man who didn't work. Her meaning came across loud and clear in her facial expressions and body language, which I interpreted as her thinking, Here is a Black man, probably lying on his butt at home, lazy, doing drugs and alcohol, cursing and beating me and taking my money, since I had a great job. I was shocked. If she hadn't been on the bench, I could have slapped her. A college educated Black man was beyond her comprehension.

After this shaky start we began the trial. One of the first things she said to me was, "You can't tell me what was said directly to you. Since I had never been in court before, my reaction was, "Huh. What do you mean?" This was direct testimony, not hearsay. I tell you what was said to me and GM can bring in their people to rebut it. GM did not produce a single witness. Magistrate Melody Anne Paige was the perfect witness for General Motors.

It was a known fact that I have Multiple Sclerosis. I received this curse while going through my apprenticeship. It did not stop me, thankfully. During the trial Magistrate Melody Paige asked the GM attorney, Benjamin Liggett, if he wanted to pursue the Roberts line of questioning. This law requires the plaintiff to reveal other jobs they are qualified to do. My attorney, Lorenzo D'Agustini, explained it to me. The GM attorney Benjamin Liggett said "No". If he had pursued the line of questioning they would have discovered that I am an *infrared* specialist. That was the job I was doing before my sadistic general foreman, Amos, sent me back to the line to be harassed again while he sat back, watched, and laughed. When Mr. Liggett said, "No," the judged looked stunned. The look she gave him seemed to say, "Help me out here a little." I was watching the exchange between them very carefully.

Benjamin Liggett said my neurologist told him I was involved in Sisterhood at Temple Israel. He wanted me to explain what Sisterhood was. Sisterhood is the women's club in the Synagogues. I joined Temple Israel Sisterhood to help serve the community. Magistrate Melody Paige's lips seemed to curl up on the sides when I revealed I was Jewish. "Wow," I thought, "she doesn't like Jews either." And here I sat before her, a Black Jew. As I sat there, I wondered what my religion had to do with my case. Hadn't she heard of Black Jews? The thought of me being Black and a Jew seemed to really trouble Ms. Paige.

Mr. Liggett decided to pursue the line of questioning me about my MS. He wanted to know when I first became aware that I have MS, who my doctor was, what were my symptoms, things that physically happened to me after my diagnosis. I answered truthfully since this was not a case of

MS. I would be a fool to file for Workers Compensation if I knew the reason I left my job was because of the MS. Magistrate Paige even wrote in her opinion that my MS was in remission. If either attorney had asked, "How much time have you missed from work because of the MS while working at the Pontiac plant?" the answer would have been "0 days."I left because drunk drugged men were threatening my life. When two of the disturbing pictures of nooses, degrading picture of a Black woman, the Biitch picture were introduced as evidence, the defense attorney's and the judge's mouths fell. It was hard evidence and they didn't know what to do with it. One picture was a horrible stereotypical nasty picture of a black woman that had been placed on the bench where I sat, and the other was a bumper sticker with the word "BIITCH" picture that was placed in my locker.

I also elaborated upon the picture described the picture was of a dead animal in the streets, titled "Roadkill." The line painters had failed to remove it because it wasn't their job. Underneath the picture these guys had printed, "Not my job Camille," because I wouldn't do their jobs while they were at the bar or on the golf course on company time. I took it as another threat to harm me.

I testified that I had seen Stan five times in one day in the department where I was working alone. He was stalking me. Magistrate Paige fraudulently wrote: "She saw the man 5 times in one week," as if I saw him casually each day walking to the time clock. When my attorney asked me if I could return to work, I replied, "Not if GM won't keep these guys off me. I will never let another man do that to me again."

I testified for about five hours in total. GM brought no one in to rebut my testimony, and I named many names. It seems they didn't need to. They had Magistrate Melody Anne Paige.

As we left Magistrate Paige's courtroom, I looked back at her. Her face was very disturbed. My attorney said he had a lot of respect for her and thought I would get a fair judgment. Judging by the look on her face, I didn't think so. What I read from her face was, "How do I help GM out of this." The law for Workers' Comp states that they have 42 days to write an opinion. It took Magistrate Paige almost eight months. My attorney told me he didn't want to prod her along because she might get mad and could retaliate. My trial was concluded on September 4, 2008. She issued her written opinion on April 17, 2009.

When I received her opinion my heart totally dropped. She not only issued the opinion against me, she omitted evidence and told so many lies her nose must have extended to the foot of Florida. I personally think she had issues with people of color, which explains her insult to my educated husband

Her ruling contained only slivers of truth. She misrepresented a memo written by a superintendent which stated that he had found a noose, removed it, and called Mike Smith of Labor Relations to inform him of his discovery. Ms. Paige wrote that I found the noose, took it down, untied it, and called Mike Smith. I don't know the area where the noose was found, never touched it, don't know who the hell Mike Smith is, and if I had found it I would never have untied it. She wrote that the union had investigated and found "No cause." I presented grievances I had written to get the UAW to help me. On the grievance there is an area called, "Supervisor's disposition." If the supervisors write "no cause," the grievance moves to a higher level. Magistrate Paige did not hear testimony from the UAW or GM, yet she wrote her opinion as if the UAW had testified. She also stated that I had called the Michigan Department of Civil Rights and she didn't understand what the call was about. I did not call the MDCR. I filed in person.

I produced paperwork that showed I had filed charges against certain supervisors, and the MDCR deemed it needed investigation. The case was transferred to the EEOC. The EEOC investigator never spoke to me but issued me a right-to-sue letter. I turned the letter over to Richard Terrell Taylor and he never filed it. Magistrate Paige also stated that there was no improvement in my mental state after I left the job. That was another lie she told to undermine Dr. Dvorkin authority. Ms. Paige wrote her opinion as if I had the mental capacity and education of a fourth grader. Ms. Paige wrote she couldn't make out the "Biitch" picture. Ray Charles could have seen the word "Biitch." In essence Magistrate Paige took my testimony and altered it in her legal opinion to give GM a win.

Once I received the liar, Magistrate Melody Paige's, opinion I was crushed. In my opinion she is the biggest liar I know. I couldn't believe the legal system was so corrupt. I could have worked under the Americans With Disabilities Act had it just been my MS, but I had guys threatening to kill me with GM's refusal to intervene. Ms. Paige wrote that my Neurologist stated that my MS was in remission in her written opinion, but she still wrote that I left the job because of my MS. I testified about Stan stalking me in court. In her opinion, Magistrate Melody Anne Paige wrote that I saw him five times that week, like I ran into him punching in or out. I testified he stalked me 5 times in one day in an isolated area threatening my life. Production was not running and I was alone in my work area. She altered the testimony in her written opinion to give GM the win.

Once I had recuperated from the initial shock I decided to confront Magistrate Paige with her lies. I autographed a copy of my previous book, the book I was selling on Amazon, the picture my daughter and me on the cover of the Jewish News, the Judges' "Code of ethics", the commandment "You will not bear false witness against your neighbor" in the King James version of the Bible, the Catholic version and the Jewish version it all read the same and I sent all three versions to her. Different Bibles don't have the same wording but mean the same. I had been a Christian for almost 50 years. Magistrate Melody Paige freaked. My Worker's Compensation attorney called to tell me not to send her anything else. I guess she viewed my confronting her with the truth as a her as a threat. She was the liar, but I told him I would not send her anything else.

A few days letter I received a letter from her boss, Christopher Ambrose, telling me it was improper to contact her. Christopher Ambrose was Chief Magistrate. Proper communication is when all parties are present. He stated that if I had concerns to contact him. The letter wasn't dated and he didn't leave a phone number. I tracked him down. He started by using his authoritative voice, I guess to intimidate me. He didn't. I had just survived males threatening to kill me, so he was nothing. I wanted questions answered about why Magistrate Paige could lie and get away with it. That reflected on his supervision. He didn't have any real answers. Mr. Ambrose contacted me directly without going through my attorney. According to his definition, his contacting me without going through my attorney was also improper communication?

In July 2010, I found out that Magistrate Paige was no longer a Workers' Comp judge after about 20 years. She had moved to Valparaiso, Indiana to take a better position with Social Security. She returned to Oak Park, MI which is my hearing office. A few months after her return to Michigan, my Social Security Disability case was called for review. I believe Melody Paige had a friend call up my case for review to cause me more harm. The timing coincided with her arrival at the office that would review my case. I had to ask my congressman to intervene. I had come to believe Melody Paige would go to any extent to cause me harm. She got a better job while I was forced to leave my job in fear of my life. I was reminded of the words of Oliver Wendell Holmes, Jr.: "This is a court of law, young man, not a court of justice."

After the what I view as a corrupt *opinion* from Magistrate Melody Anne Paige, my attorney filed an appeal in May 2009. The case was heard by Magistrates Murray A. Gorchow, James P. Harvey, and Gregory Przybylo. Judges Gorchow and Harvey were in favor of sending it back to remand. They wanted to know if my claim was "grounded in reality or not." That was what they wrote. Magistrate Gregory Przybylo simply stated that Magistrate Melody Paige's opinion should be taken as is. That's not an appeal. That sounds like an easy paycheck for Magistrate Przybylo. The case was remanded to Magistrate Michael Mason for review. He stated that he found me a very credible witness and all I had stated was founded in reality. Unfortunately, he stated that I had left the job due to my MS without proof. GM did not have the proper paperwork stating I left the job on October 17, 2003 because of MS. They only had the psychologist's paperwork stating that he had removed me from the hostile work environment where my life was threatened by another drugged out man. It took a year-and-a-half to send it back to remand and another year for the answer. "Remand" in Worker's Compensation cases means the judge's opinion is sent back to them for further clarification or consideration.

Two judges were replaced on the Workers' Comp court by Governor Rick Snyder. Magistrate Przybylo got to to write the lead opinion. He was already against me in the first appeal. He stated that they should just go with Magistrate Melody Paige's Opinion and now that he got his opportunity to write lead opinion for the appeal. I didn't stand a chance. He wrote that Magistrate Mason didn't fully answer all the questions and without those questions answered there was "no proof" to support my claim. How was that my fault? The Board or Worker's Compensation appellate court denied my claim and I filed another claim with The Michigan Court of Appeals which is the next step. In my view these judges are worse than criminals on the street. They lie, cheat, destroy lives, all under the cover of a law degree. With two denials at the lower level I didn't stand a chance with the courts, but I tried anyway.

May 28, 2012 I was preparing my Shabbat dinner and heard knocking on my door. I yelled,"

"Who is it?"

A voice said, "FBI."

"Hold On"

I grabbed my walker and made it to the front door. When I opened the door, there were two agents standing there.

"Do you know Melody Paige?"

"Yes." I rolled my eyes, unable to hide my disdain for her.

Apparently someone had been sending her negative information. She had returned to Michigan and began work as a Social Security law judge in Oak Park, Michigan.

ODAR stands for Office of Disability Adjudication and Review.

The FBI said to me. "Well, she thinks you did it. Do you know anyone who would?"

"If she lied on me I'm quite sure she lied on others."

"I'm sure the New Black Panthers would not like me. I'm Jewish."

"Well, she didn't say this but did you see your attorney in the streets and approach him?", the agent said.

"No, I did see the GM attorney at a local restaurant but didn't say anything to him."

"Melody Paige said she believes you got a raw deal but she had to base her judgment on the evidence presented."

"We have to move this to homeland security."

Whatever, I thought and just looked at him. I knew he was trying to scare me but I hadn't done anything.

I figured out what the FBI meant about approaching the attorney. I saw my corrupt attorney Richard Terrell Taylor at a restaurant in Royal Oak, MI, and approached him about filing my appeal. I wrote it in the previous book, which I sent Magistrate Melody Anne Paige. I had every right to approach and ask Mr. Taylor about my appeal. He was still my current attorney.

Melody Anne Paige now works at the ODAR office in Oak park, MI. I feel sorry for Detroit claimants. If you look ODAR (Oak Park) Melody Paige her name appears as an administrative law judge along with comments about her. I'm not the only one she messed over. Apparently, her track record with Black America is not good. It seems an attorney may have posted this on the Disabilityjudge.com concerning Ms. Paige. This is exactly what was written. Just because they're an attorney doesn't mean they can spell.

"She is definitely rude and disrespecful to my African American clients. She implies they are lying and her demeanor is one of superiority and distrust. Its too bad we have someone like that hearing disability cases. She forgets these claimant's are not criminals."

On May 20, 2013, I contacted my attorney Worker's Compensation. He let me know the Michigan Court of Appeals had refused to hear my case.

I filed an appeal with the Michigan Supreme Court around June 24, 2013. On October 11, 2013, I learned that the MI Supreme Court had denied my appeal. The first Workers' Compensation magistrate, Melody Anne Paige, lied about me and every other judge or magistrate rubber stamped her corrupt opinion.

Derek called me in March, 2012. He wanted to invite my husband and me out to dinner with him and the girl he was seeing then. I chuckled to myself. He thought it was okay to have dinner with the man whose wife he was hounding for sex and helping her lose her job. Derek had a very warped mind, indeed. I don't know what he thought I would see in him if I had been single. He was half the size of my husband, shorter than me, low educated, had nasty teeth to name a few negative things about him. He was a runt. He was very disrespectful to us Black women. He thought that function of Black women in life was to relieve his sexual needs and receptacles for his seed. There was nothing about him that would ever attract me.

"Do you remember the day I broke my hand, he asked?"

"Like I would ever forget", I said.

"I was on a really bad drug that day. That's why I punched the locker."

"I knew you were on something. That's why I told you to leave."

After I left the job, Derek started dating and sleeping with a security guard who worked at the plant. His mentality never changed. The plants are referred to as "meat markets" and Derek ran up an expensive bill in the meat department. If I had been weak and given in to Derek, I believe he would have tried to commit perverse acts on me to prove his dominance over me when he bragged to the guys. I was able to send him a Facebook message telling him about the awful way he treated me.

I would rather live with the devastating effects of MS than live one day with the reminder that I slept with him. I lost my job, My MS is now progressive and I can't walk. I have weird sensations throughout my body because of the progressive MS. I have numbness throughout my body. I can only sleep four or five hours a night because of these sensations. The medicine I take does little to help. I'm glad I left because our work relationship was getting darker. Derek, Amos and LeRoy were three of four of the worst Black males I have ever encountered. The other was Sam the nasty drunk at American Axle who I fought with in the manlift.

In summary, LeRoy, who I felt was very ignorant, tried to control me and kept making comments about my body. Amos tried to control me and force his form of religion on me; and Derek tried to control me and force me to sleep with him. None of them had that right. Derek was intent on exerting complete control over me. The more I said "NO," the worse our work relationship became and it was only a matter of time before one of us got hurt. It's not that I was irresistible, but I was female. Derek was high the majority of the time. There is no way he can recall all the things he said and did to me and he did a lot. His pursuit of sex with me was growing stronger each day. Maybe if GM managers had focused their attention on GM products instead of focusing on me because I didn't listen to non-skilled male employees tell me how to do my job, maybe they would not have had to recall millions of poorly manufactured cars.

The UAW is trying to recruit southern plants to become UAW members. So far they have not been successful. What happened to me is what the workers can expect if they vote "in" the UAW. The Canadians split from the UAW in 1984 and formed the Canadian Auto workers (CAW). The UAW promoted Chad through the ranks with all the baggage he carried. He stole materials from General Motors, had his card punched when he wasn't there, harassed me horribly and sent other guys like Stan to harass me more because I wouldn't allow Chad to use me. This is what I received from the UAW, the institution that was in charge of protecting me. I wrote to many top union officials, including Union President, Bob King, begging for their help. They ignored me. I wish I had my union dues back. Workers should know from my story what to expect from UAW "representation".

We need ways to get judges to disqualify themselves from cases where they obviously have exhibited extreme bias toward one litigant. Judge McDonald severed the class action suit, and then used his corrupt court-room to dispose of all the cases. Cases should be filtered to all judges in the interest of fairness. One judge controlled all the GM cases in the Class Action lawsuit. Other judges may have a different thought process. Fifteen people can't all be wrong. Judge McDonald seemed determined that there would be no action taken against GM and stated that my only form of redress was Workers Comp. Apparently, he didn't know the law concern-ing intentional torts. I had the right to bring civil action on all the charges. In my opinion, Magistrate Melody Anne Paige intentionally destroyed my out-of-court settlement. She lied, ignored evidence, manufactured evi-dence, altered evidence, suppressed evidence, came to her own medical conclusions, and did not properly conduct herself as an honorable judge. I have been left with no course of redress except to tell the truth in this book. My case cries out for justice and reform of our judicial system. Judge McDonald denied me "due process" and "access to the courts." Magistrate Melody Paige just told outright lies. To not get my story out rewards those who seem to be crooked "officers of the court." The officers are not held accountable because no one knows they are corrupt.

If I could hit the rewind button on this situation I would never have approached the UAW or GM for help. The UAW took six years of union dues from me while failing to represent me. Taking gripes to court is a joke. The judges discriminated against me because I am afflicted with Multiple Sclerosis. I went through about nineteen Michigan judges. Only two seemed willing to follow the law, the rest just seemed to back GM. If your name is GM you can get away with anything, but they couldn't stop me from writing a book. If GM attorneys had abided by our out-of-court settlement I wouldn't have the freedom to write this book.